WORKS

In the Home

Contents

Introduction

Living in a house these days is so different from what it used to be. Not so very long ago houses were very cold, dark and drafty places to live in. People often had to carry water to their homes in buckets from an outdoor pump; and there were no machines to help them cook, wash and mend. What a difference there is today.

The modern home has a host of machines, devices and gadgets to help us save time, make us more comfortable and entertain us. It is only perhaps when they break down that we

realize that life in the home has become quite complicated!

We all know *what* these domestic devices do, but most of us find *how* they do it rather mysterious. How often have you said to yourself, "I wonder how it works?" This book has the answers. It solves most of the mysteries that lurk around the house. It takes you behind the scenes and reveals the plumbing and wiring. It tells you how the common household equipment and appliances work, and shows you what they are like inside.

Servicing Your Home

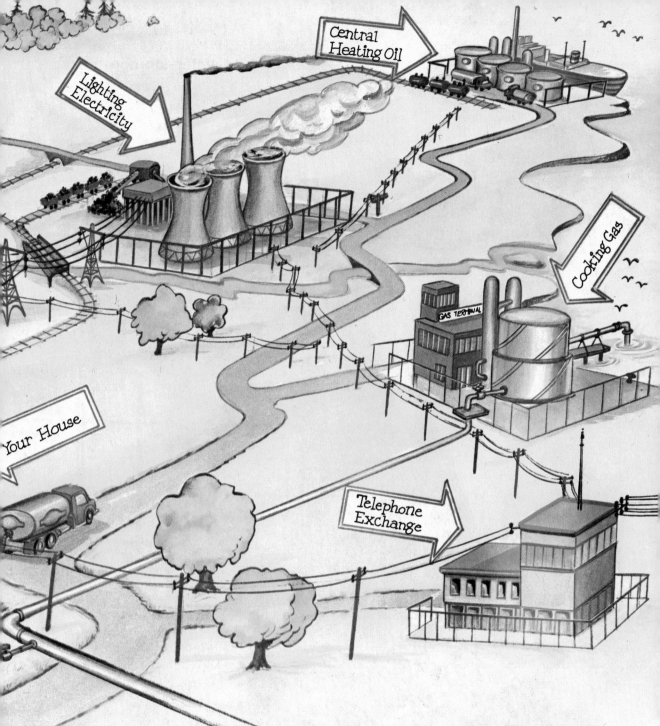

Hundreds of people work in industries that provide services to your house. At the power station they make electricity to light your lights and drive your machines. At the refinery they produce oil for your central heating boilers. At the gas plant they supply gas for cooking. At the water treatment plant they pump water from reservoirs and make it fit to drink. At the sewage works they treat your waste water and sewage to make it harmless. At the telephone exchange they put through your telephone calls. At the broadcasting station they produce radio and television programs to inform and entertain you.

9

Cold water storage tanks

Hot water system

Radiator

Electric lighting circuit

10

Behind the Scenes

It takes a long time to build a house. First you have to find a suitable piece of land, or building plot. Then you have to buy it. Next you ask an architect to design and draw up detailed plans of the house you want to build. These plans must then go to the planning department of the local government authority. If they approve your design, they will pass your plans and allow you to go ahead.

Next you must find a builder to build your house. He orders all the materials you will need – bricks, cement, sand, gravel, tiles, lumber, window frames, doors and so on. The builder may sometimes do all the work himself, but usually he calls in other craftsmen to help him. Bricklayers build the inner and outer walls of bricks, mortar and concrete blocks. Carpenters fit the windows, doors and timbers for the roof. Tilers lay the tiles. Together they construct the main skeleton of the house.

When those craftsmen have finished, others take their place. Plumbers move in with copper piping, taps, radiators and other fittings and install the water supply and central heating system. Electricians are meanwhile putting in the wiring, switches, sockets and fuses for the electric lighting and power systems. If you had X-ray eyes, you would be amazed at the amount of piping and wiring you would see in your house – hundreds of yards of it.

Plasterers follow the plumbers and electricians to finish the walls and ceilings. They cover the wires and fill any holes the earlier people have made. Painters follow the plasterers to make your new home colorful and help protect it from the weather. When the painters move out, you can move in.

Electric power circuit

Central heating boiler

Plumbing

We use an enormous amount of water in our homes, often as much as 50 gallons (200 liters) a day. We use only a small amount for drinking and cooking. Most is used for washing, bathing and flushing the toilet. Most homes take their water from the mains – a large pipe that runs beneath the road outside. It is piped into your house by way of a large tap, or stopcock. Inside your house the water travels through a maze of pipes to storage tanks and boilers, shower and toilet, sink and wash basin. The waste water leaves through a network of other pipes, which connect with the outside drains.

The plumbing system in a house includes all the pipework and fittings of the hot and cold water supply and drainage systems. The word "plumbing" comes from the Latin word for lead. In the past lead was used for the piping.

In many houses the plumbing also includes the pipework and fittings of the central heating system. These can be seen under the "Heating" section of this book, beginning on page 30.

Joints, Taps and Traps

The maze of pipework that forms the plumbing system of a house is made up of many lengths of pipe joined together. There are straight joints and joints that go around corners. These joints are made with fittings having such names as elbows, tees and y's, depending on their shape.

Plumbers use several different methods to join pipes. The neatest way to join copper pipes is by soldering. Solder is a metal that melts easily and quickly hardens. Plumbers solder pipes using what is called a capillary joint. First they fit the ends of the pipes into a copper sleeve. Then they melt solder on to the joint using a gas torch or blowlamp. The thin space between the sleeve and the pipe draws in the solder, which then cools and hardens.

Another way of joining copper pipes is by a compression joint. The pipes are fitted into a brass sleeve which has screw threads on the outside. Watertight joints are made with soft copper rings (unions). These are compressed, or squeezed between the pipes and the sleeve when the nuts on the sleeve are tightened.

To control the flow of water through and out of the pipes there are valves and taps. The ordinary tap over a sink or wash basin screws on to the water supply pipe. When you turn the tap on, water flows through a hole in the tap body and out through the spout. When you turn the tap off, you screw down a rubber washer on to a seat and block up the hole.

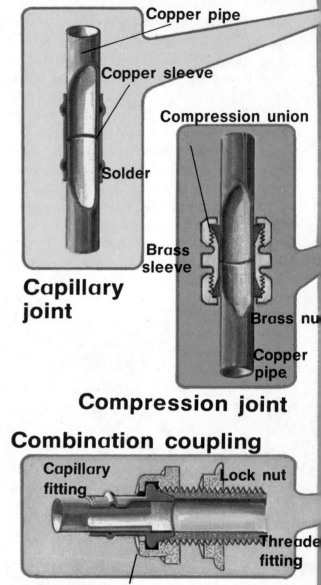

Copper pipe

Copper sleeve

Solder

Capillary joint

Compression union

Brass sleeve

Brass nut

Copper pipe

Compression joint

Combination coupling

Capillary fitting

Lock nut

Threaded fitting

Brass compression nut

In some kitchens mixer taps are used. These have hot and cold water taps in the same unit, with a single outlet spout. The hot and cold water can be mixed to give the temperature you want.

If you look at the pipe that carries waste water from the sink, you notice

Drains

that it is bent double. This is done to trap water in the bottom. Such a trap prevents smells from the drains getting into the house. In some waste pipes there is a waste disposal unit which shreds waste food so that it can pass through the pipe.

Water main

Elbow joints

Sink unit

Tap

Packing gland

Washer

Spout

Seating

Trap

Splash baffle

Static blades

Rotating blades

Waste disposal unit

Electric motor

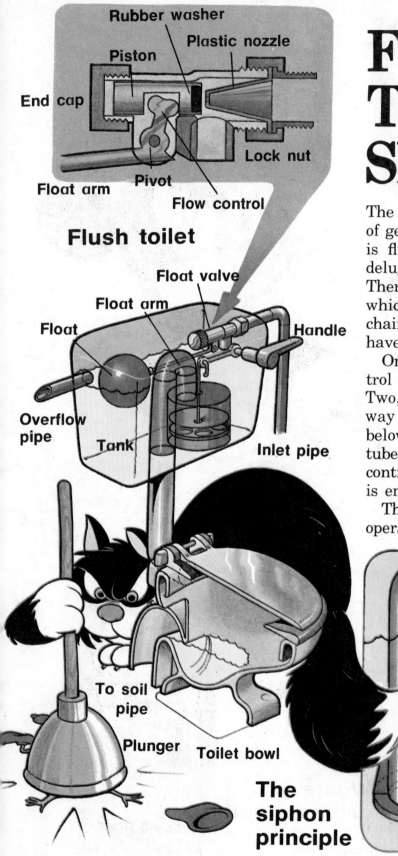

Rubber washer

Plastic nozzle

Piston

End cap

Float arm

Pivot

Flow control

Lock nut

Flush toilet

Float valve

Float arm

Float

Handle

Overflow pipe

Tank

Inlet pipe

To soil pipe

Plunger

Toilet bowl

The siphon principle

Inlet ports

Water inlet

Rubber diaphragm valve

Flush Toilet and Shower

The flush toilet is a very hygienic way of getting rid of body waste. The waste is flushed from the toilet bowl in a deluge of water from a tank above it. There are various kinds of tanks, which may be worked by handles, chains, buttons or levers, but they all have two things in common.

One, they have a float valve to control the flow of water into the tank. Two, they work by siphon action. One way a siphon works is shown in the box below. Once water is flowing through a tube from a high to a low level, it continues to flow until the upper tank is empty.

The picture shows a low-level tank operated by a handle. The handle is attached to a piston inside a cylinder. The bottom of the cylinder is open, and from the top a pipe goes up, over and down to join the pipe going to the bowl. When the tank is full, the water fills the cylinder, but the down pipe is empty.

When you press the handle, the piston rises and lifts water through the up pipe, over and through the down pipe. This starts the siphon action, and water continues to flow until the tank is empty.

As the tank empties, the float valve opens and allows water to flow in through the inlet pipe. It is called a float valve because it is worked by a hollow ball that floats on the surface of the water. When the water level drops, the float drops too and levers the valve washer away from the inlet nozzle. As the tank fills, the float rises and eventually levers the washer back against the nozzle.

Shower head

To shower head

Shower

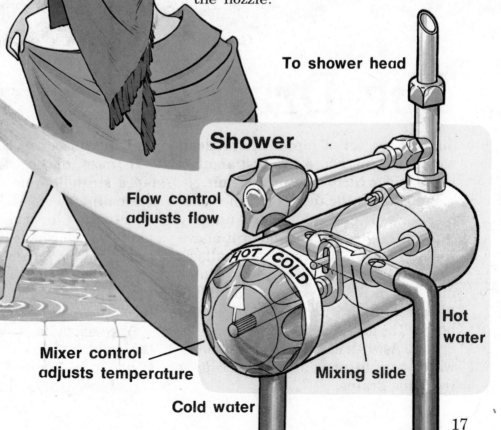

**Flow control
adjusts flow**

HOT / COLD

**Mixer control
adjusts temperature**

Mixing slide

**Hot
water**

Cold water

17

The water from the gulley and that from the soil pipe is channeled separately through stoneware pipes into an inspection chamber, or manhole. The pipes are glazed, or have a glassy coating. This stops the water getting out. The pipes are joined by means of concrete. The manhole is a pit lined with concrete and covered with an iron lid. The water flows through the manhole in open channels. They are open so

Plunger

Waste pipe

Water trap

Gulley

Grating

Inspection chamber

Cover

Soil pipe inlet

The Drainage System

Just as one set of pipes carries clean water into the house, so must another set of pipes carry dirty water out.

Water from the toilet is flushed into a large soil pipe, which goes directly into the ground. At the top of it above roof level is an open vent, which allows gases to escape. Other waste water may also go into the soil pipe, or it may be piped into a gulley outside the house. The gulley leads into the outside drains. As with all waste pipes, it has a water trap to prevent gases escaping from the drains.

that the pipes can be cleaned.

In most towns the waste water is piped straight from the manhole into the main sewer. The sewer carries it eventually to a sewage treatment plant, which cleans it. In many country areas, however, there is no main sewerage, so houses must have another system. This can be a cesspool or a septic tank.

A cesspool is a huge underground tank which stores all the waste water. It has to be emptied regularly by special tanker trucks, fitted with powerful suction pumps. The septic tank, however, is a miniature sewage treatment plant. It often consists of two large tanks. The waste water flows into the first tank, and the solid matter it contains falls to the bottom, forming a sludge. The clearer water passes into the second tank and filters through some gravelly material. This removes any solid bits remaining. The water next flows into a drainage area made up of gravel, from which it soaks away into the ground. Septic tanks do not need to be emptied very often because the sludge gradually breaks down and passes from the system.

In rainy weather, a great deal of water runs off the roof of the house. This is collected by gutters or rainspouts. It passes through down pipes to pipes leading to a drainage area or to sewers called storm drains.

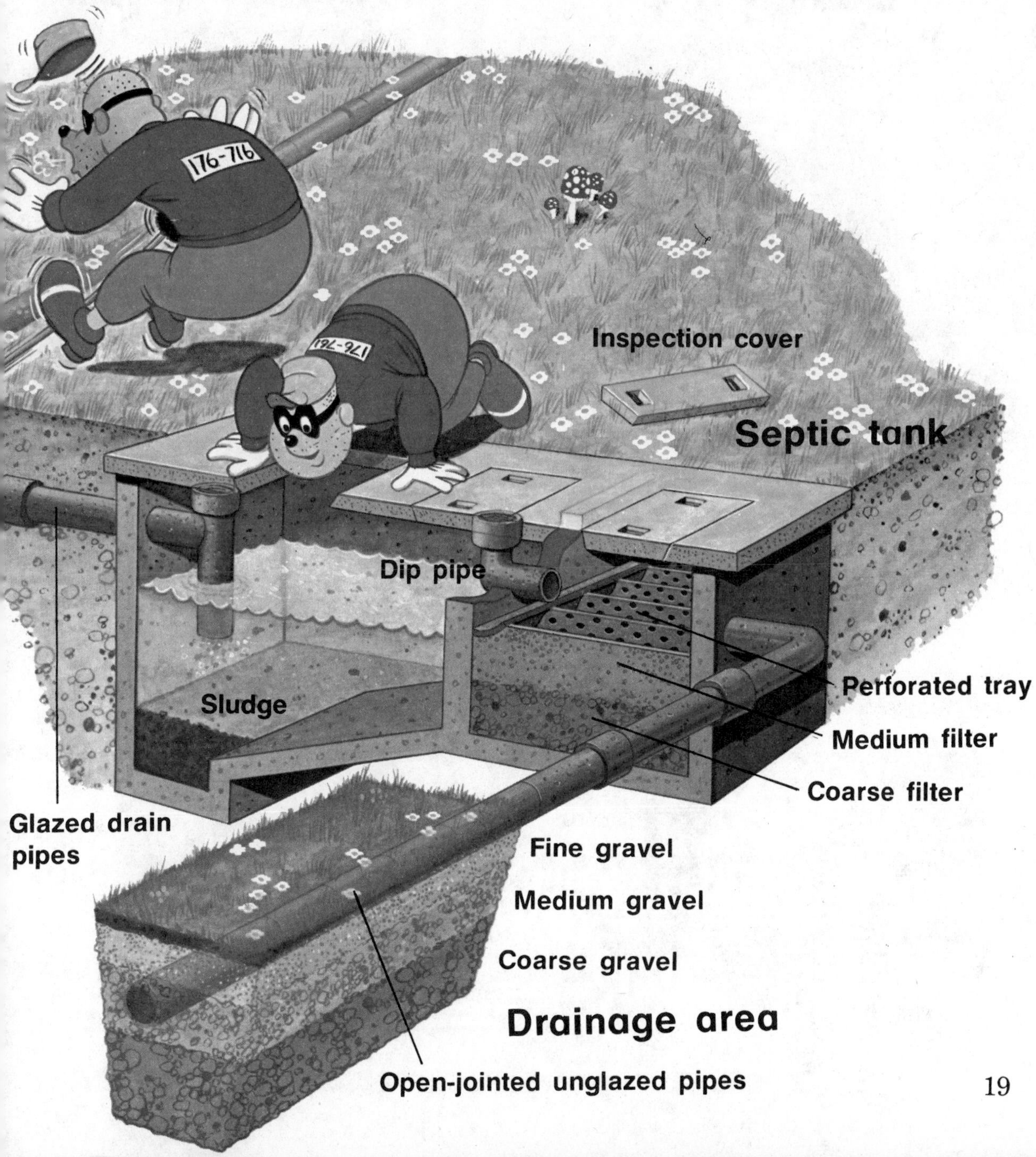

Inspection cover

Septic tank

Dip pipe

Perforated tray

Medium filter

Coarse filter

Sludge

Glazed drain pipes

Fine gravel

Medium gravel

Coarse gravel

Drainage area

Open-jointed unglazed pipes

Light

Light

Hot water heater

Heater switch

Switch

Switch

Vacuum cleaner

Light

Light

Switch

Switch

Junction and fusebox

Electric meter

Electric outlet

Electric stove

Electric outlet

Electric cable from street

Home Electricity

Electric outlet

Light

Cord switch

Electric drill

Electric outlet

Hundreds of yards of copper wiring weave through the walls, the floors and the ceilings of your home. The wires carry the most convenient form of energy man has yet produced – electricity.

Life became a lot brighter and a lot easier when man learned to make and transmit electricity in the 1800s. An Italian, Alessandro Volta, first discovered how to produce electricity in 1800 when he made a battery. We still remember him by measuring the strength of electricity in "volts." In 1831 the English scientist Michael Faraday built a machine that could produce electricity continuously. It was the forerunner of the powerful generators that supply electricity to our homes today.

Throughout the book you will notice the enormous number of machines in the home that are powered by electricity. Many other kinds of machines outside the home are electrically powered. Sometimes it happens when everyone is using more electricity than usual, the power stations may not be able to supply enough. Then we suffer from "blackouts," with large areas having their electricity supply cut off. It is then that we appreciate just how much we have come to rely on electricity.

Measuring Electricity

Electricity is made in a power station by an electricity generator. It travels across the country to our homes through thick cables (transmission lines) carried on tall steel towers (pylons). It passes into our homes by way of an overhead or underground cable and then splits into a number of paths (circuits) in a junction box, or fusebox. These circuits feed the lights, the stove, the water heater and so on.

Before it goes to the fusebox the electricity passes through a meter which measures the amount of electricity your home takes in and uses. As it flows through the meter, the electric current makes the meter dials move. One dial shows the number of units of electricity; the others show tens of units, hundreds of units, thousands of units and so on.

From time to time someone comes to read the meter. He notes down the position of the pointers on the dials. This will be different from the last time he read the meter. The difference between the two sets of readings gives the number of units of electricity used in your home since the last reading. Soon you will receive a bill charging you for that amount of electricity.

Apart from the dials, the other main thing you notice about an electric meter is the aluminum disc, or rotor. This turns when you use electricity. The disc is positioned between two electromagnets. These are pieces of iron which have coils wound around them. When electricity flows through the coils, the pieces of iron become magnets. Their magnetism makes the disc spin around.

The disc is mounted on a spindle which has gear teeth on the end. These mesh with the teeth on gearwheels that drive the dials around. When the disc turns, the dials also turn.

After passing through the meter, the electricity goes into the fusebox. From this box wires carry electricity to different parts of the house. The electricity passes into these wires through a fuse. This is a thin wire which melts if too much electricity passes through it. It prevents too much electricity flowing in a circuit, which could set the house on fire.

Meter reader

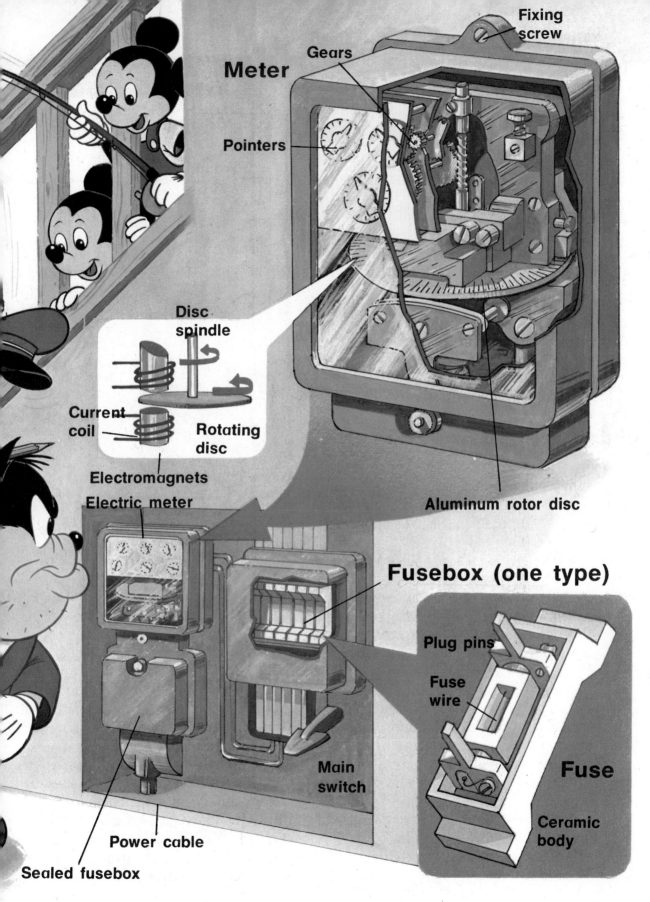

Meter

Fixing screw

Gears

Pointers

Disc spindle

Current coil

Rotating disc

Electromagnets

Aluminum rotor disc

Electric meter

Fusebox (one type)

Plug pins

Fuse wire

Fuse

Ceramic body

Main switch

Power cable

Sealed fusebox

Dimmer switch

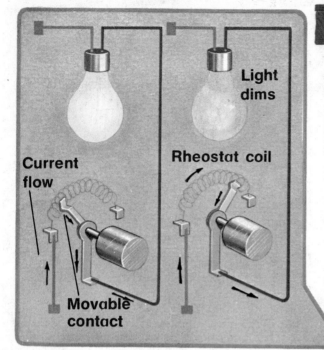

Light
dims

Rheostat coil

Current
flow

Movable
contact

Live
wire

Light
fixture

Ground
wire

Plugging In

Many older homes and apartments are not adequately wired for the wide variety and number of electric appliances we have today.

Electricity comes into the house from electric cables, which are multistranded wires. It travels through the meter (see previous page) and flows through wires to various parts of the house by different paths, or circuits. From these circuits, power is drawn through outlets or receptacles, sometimes called sockets. Overloading circuits with too many appliances can overheat wiring and cause fires.

We measure electric current in units called amps or ampères. The measurement is 1 amp per second.

Amps flow along the wire because of pressure measured by volts.

Watts are units of measuring the electric power used by each appliance

and lighting fixture. Before plugging an appliance into an outlet, you should know how much power the motor will need to operate properly to be sure that particular circuit can handle it.

Most outlet and switch boxes are metal, with holes or partially loosened "knock-outs" on the back and side through which to attach wires and cables. The wires and cables are clamped in, the box is attached into the wall and a switchplate or outlet cover

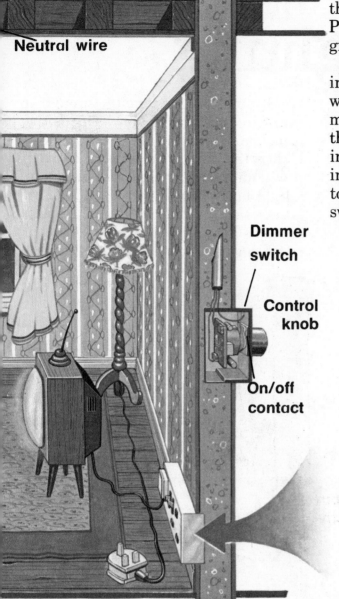

Neutral wire

Dimmer switch

Control knob

On/off contact

the appliance or lamp is switched off. Plugs should be pulled out of sockets by grasping the plug.

The ends, or terminals, of the wires in outlets, switches, plugs and other wiring devices are color-coded and must be attached properly to provide the flow of electricity from the circuit into the socket. The plug makes contact in the socket to provide the electricity to the appliance or lamp when it is switched on.

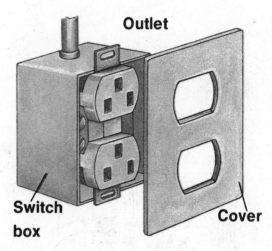

Outlet

Switch box

Cover

is put in place, sealing the box.

The modern wall socket has 3 openings: 2 parallel slots for the twin blades of the plug, and a third, round hole. The function of the round hole and plug pin that fits into it is to "ground" the appliance or tool. Grounding is an important safety measure, to protect the user from getting an electric shock.

Plugs have prongs which match the openings in electric outlets. Appliances and lamps should be plugged in when

As well as ordinary light switches (see next page), you can fit dimmer switches into the lighting circuits. One type has a resistance coil, or rheostat. By bringing more of the coil into the circuit, through a movable contact, you reduce the flow of electric current and the lights dim. Another kind of dimmer switch uses a kind of crystal called a thyristor to reduce the electric current.

Electric Lighting

Light bulb

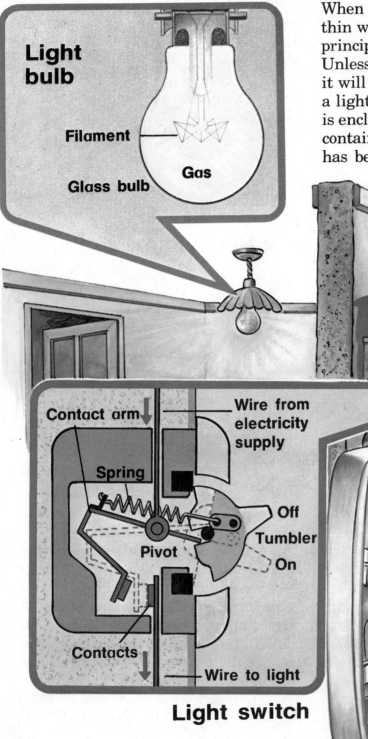

Filament

Gas

Glass bulb

When you pass electricity through a thin wire, it starts to glow. This is the principle behind the electric light bulb. Unless the wire is protected, however, it will quickly burn up in the air. So in a light bulb the thin wire, or filament, is enclosed in a glass bulb, and the bulb contains air from which all the oxygen has been removed. Then the filament

Contact arm

Wire from electricity supply

Spring

Off

Tumbler

On

Pivot

Contacts

Wire to light

Light switch

Fluorescent lamp

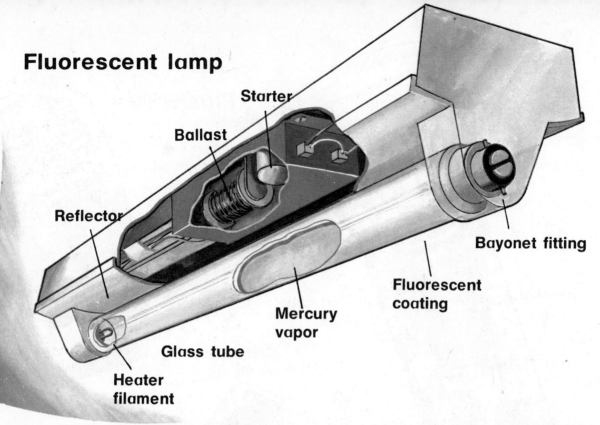

Starter

Ballast

Reflector

Bayonet fitting

Fluorescent coating

Mercury vapor

Glass tube

Heater filament

does not burn up. A metal called tungsten is used for the filament because it remains strong even when it gets hot.

The wires lead from the filament to contacts at the base of the bulb. These press against matching spring contacts in the bulb socket. Then the bulb screws into the socket. When the lamp or fixture is turned on, the power flows from the socket through the contact on the bulb and the bulb lights.

In the kitchen another kind of light may be used – the fluorescent lamp. This is a long tube containing vapor of the liquid metal mercury. It is coated on the inside with a special material. When electricity is passed through the tube, the atoms of mercury in the vapor start to glow. They also give off invisible ultraviolet rays.

When these rays hit the coating on the tube, they cause it to glow. The glow of the atoms of vapor and of the coating produces a pleasant "soft" light much like daylight. Another word for "glow" is fluorescence. That is why we call this kind of lamp a fluorescent lamp.

A ballast and starter are needed to start the tube. They work together when the lamp is first switched on to provide a pulse of high-voltage electricity which makes the vapor begin to glow.

We turn on the lights with a flick of a switch. The usual type of switch is the toggle switch. It is shown on the left in the "off" position. In this position no electricity can flow between the wire carrying the electricity in and the wire leading to the light, because the contacts are open. When you push the switch down into the "on" position (dotted lines), the contact arm snaps down and presses the contacts together. Current can then flow through the switch and to the light.

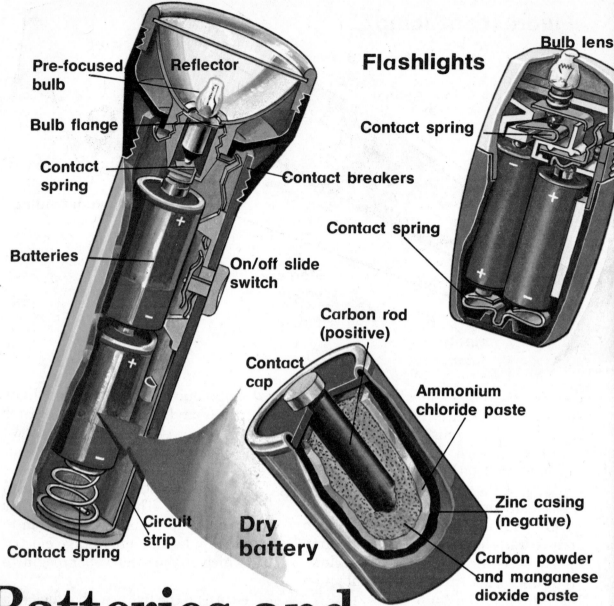

Pre-focused bulb

Reflector

Flashlights

Bulb lens

Bulb flange

Contact spring

Contact spring

Contact spring

Batteries

Contact breakers

On/off slide switch

Carbon rod (positive)

Contact cap

Ammonium chloride paste

Circuit strip

Dry battery

Zinc casing (negative)

Contact spring

Carbon powder and manganese dioxide paste

Batteries and Flashlights

Batteries provide us with a portable source of electricity – one we can carry around with us.

Most of the batteries we use are known as dry cell batteries. They are called "dry" because they don't use liquid materials. The early batteries did use liquids and were very messy to work with. Some kinds of modern batteries also use liquids. Car batteries do, for example. They are made up of lead plates in a solution of sulphuric acid.

Every battery makes use of what is called electrochemistry. Inside the battery, chemical reactions take place which produce electricity. A battery can be made simply by putting two rods

or plates of different metals into a chemical solution. When you connect the two metals, electricity flows from one to the other.

We call the solution between the electrodes, the electrolyte. The metal rods or plates are called electrodes. We call one the positive and the other the negative. The current flows from the positive (+) to the negative (−).

In the ordinary dry battery the positive electrode is a rod of carbon. It is positioned in the center of the battery, and has a brass cap on the top. The negative electrode is zinc. It forms the casing of the battery. The electrolyte is a wet paste of powdered carbon called ammonium chloride. A paste of powdered carbon and manganese dioxide surrounds the carbon rod. This mixture removes tiny bubbles of gas which form on the rod. If the gas were allowed to build up, it would prevent the electricity from flowing.

Fortunately batteries are much easier to use than to explain! They can be fitted into flashlights, radios and so on, in a few seconds. When you are putting in two or more batteries, always make sure that the positive (+) of one battery is in contact with the negative (−) of the other. If the two + or two − electrodes are touching, no electricity will flow.

The illustrations show two common kinds of flashlights, an ordinary hand flashlight and pocket flashlight. The hand flashlight has a reflector to concentrate the light from the bulb into a strong beam. The pocket flashlight does not have a reflector. It has a tiny lens in the top.

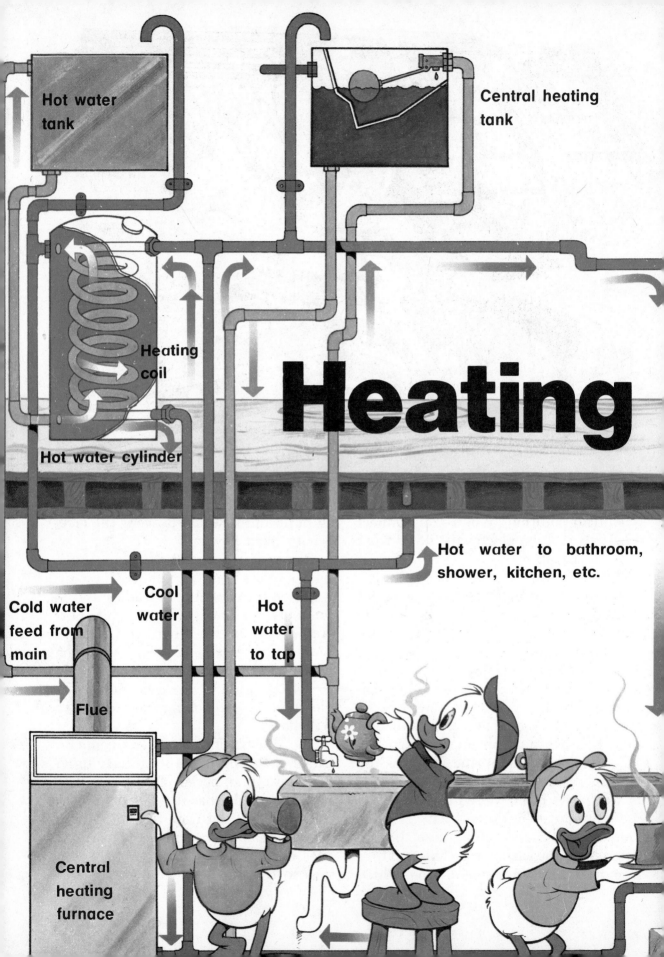

Hot water tank

Central heating tank

Heating coil

Hot water cylinder

Heating

Hot water to bathroom, shower, kitchen, etc.

Cold water feed from main

Cool water

Hot water to tap

Flue

Central heating furnace

Unless you happen to live in a very warm climate, your house will need to be heated for part of the year; and even when it doesn't need to be heated, you will need hot water for washing and cleaning.

In some houses the only form of heating was by means of open fires. Open fires look very cozy, but much of the heat they produce goes up the chimney and is lost. Modern houses have more efficient central heating systems, in which fuel is burned in a furnace. Much less heat is lost. The central heating system heats not only the rooms in the house, but also the hot water.

Houses without central heating use other methods of heating. They may use stoves that burn coal or wood; or gas, electric or kerosene heaters. To heat water they may have an electric or a gas heater.

Radiator

Control valve

Back to furnace

Plumber

Heating with Oil

Many central heating systems are powered by an oil burner. This burns an oil which is not as heavy as car engine oil nor as light as kerosene, but something in between.

The oil is fed to the boiler from an outside storage tank. This is filled up by tanker trucks which transport the oil from the nearest oil refinery. An oil level gauge tells you how much oil remains in the tank. In some systems, the oil is piped from the tank into the house to a control tank near the boiler. A ball valve ensures that there is a constant level of oil in the tank. It is operated by a float, as in a toilet tank (see page 16).

From the control tank the oil goes through a regulating valve to the burner. As it touches the hot sides of the burner it vaporizes, or turns to vapor. The vapor then burns in the combustion chamber and continues burning while the oil supply is maintained. The air needed for burning, or combustion, enters through holes at the base of the burner. Often a fan is fitted to blow the air into the combustion chamber. In the model shown here some of the air passes around the combustion chamber and is thereby warmed. It comes out through an outlet duct to heat the room.

The combustion chamber is surrounded by a jacket containing water. As the oil burns, the water becomes hot. It travels up into the heat exchanger in the hot water cylinder and then returns to the boiler. In the heat exchanger it heats up the water

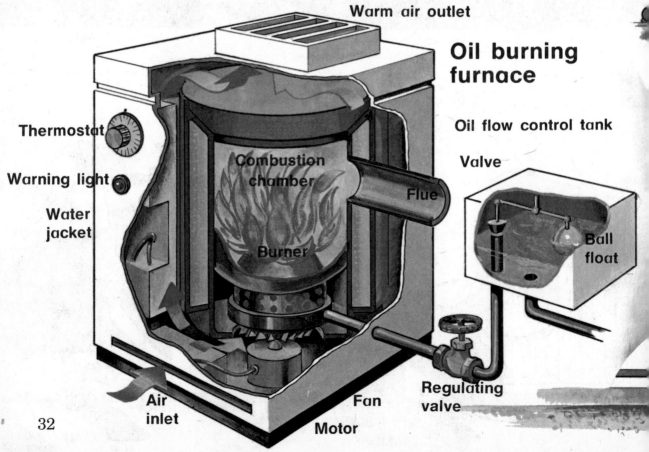

Warm air outlet

Oil burning furnace

Thermostat

Warning light

Water jacket

Combustion chamber

Burner

Flue

Oil flow control tank

Valve

Ball float

Air inlet

Fan

Motor

Regulating valve

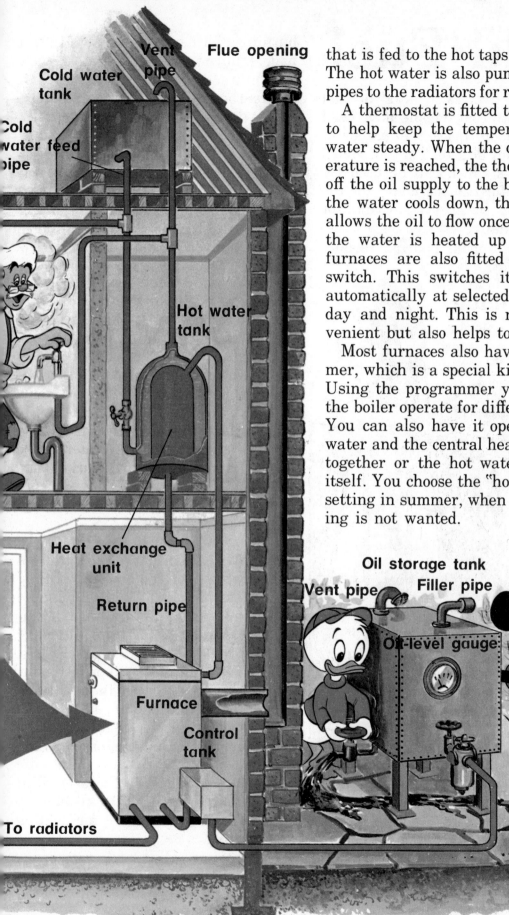

Cold water tank

Vent pipe

Flue opening

Cold water feed pipe

Hot water tank

Heat exchange unit

Return pipe

Furnace

Control tank

To radiators

Oil storage tank

Filler pipe

Vent pipe

Oil-level gauge

that is fed to the hot taps in the house. The hot water is also pumped through pipes to the radiators for room heating.

A thermostat is fitted to the furnace to help keep the temperature of the water steady. When the desired temperature is reached, the thermostat cuts off the oil supply to the burner. When the water cools down, the thermostat allows the oil to flow once more so that the water is heated up again. Most furnaces are also fitted with a time switch. This switches it on and off automatically at selected times of the day and night. This is not only convenient but also helps to save fuel.

Most furnaces also have a programmer, which is a special kind of switch. Using the programmer you can make the boiler operate for different periods. You can also have it operate the hot water and the central heating systems together or the hot water system by itself. You choose the "hot water only" setting in summer, when central heating is not wanted.

Solid Fuel

Oil is a relatively new kind of fuel compared with coal. People have been burning coal on fires for hundreds of years, and they do still. They also burn coal in stoves which can be used for cooking and for heating water for the domestic hot water system and for central heating.

A modern central heating furnace burning a form of coal is shown on this page. It burns a very pure coal we know as anthracite. Anthracite is almost pure carbon. It is shiny and quite clean to the touch. It also gives out much more heat than ordinary coal when it burns.

Other stoves or boilers burn another form of solid fuel – coke. Coke is coal which has been heated fiercely out of contact with the air. When this is done, gases are given off and what remains is a light, porous mass we call coke.

In the solid fuel furnace shown, anthracite is fed slowly to the fire grate from a storage bin. It burns in a controlled supply of air provided by an electric fan, or blower. The amount of air blown in is controlled by a thermostat, or heat switch. The faster the air is blown in, the more fiercely the anthracite burns and the faster the heat is given out. The water to be heated is contained in a jacket surrounding the furnace flue, through which the hot gases pass on their way to the chimney.

Ash from the fire drops through the grate into an ash pan. Often the ash particles fuse, or combine together to form a solid mass. This is removed from time to time by pulling a lever, which causes it to fall into the pan.

Compared with oil and gas boilers, solid fuel boilers are more trouble. They have to be fed by hand at least once a day in the winter, and the ash pan has to be emptied regularly. Also, space must be found to store the fuel. On the other hand there is more solid fuel in the world than there is oil or gas. So one day we might all have to change back to solid fuel for heating and cooking.

Coal furnace

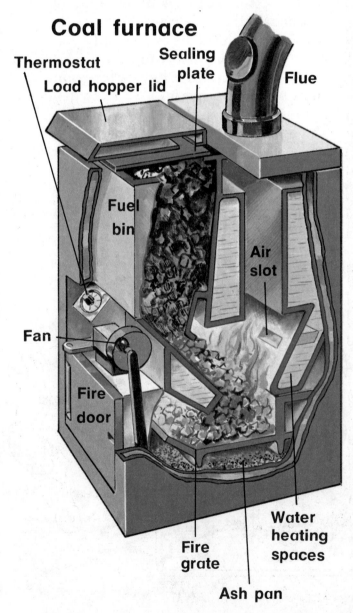

Thermostat

Load hopper lid

Sealing plate

Flue

Fuel bin

Air slot

Fan

Fire door

Fire grate

Water heating spaces

Ash pan

One of the best solid fuel stoves made for cooking is shown here. The fuel is burned slowly in a well-insulated section made of heavy iron. It has both a fast-cooking and a slow-cooking oven, together with hot plates for both slow cooking and fast cooking. Heavy lids over the hot plates keep them hot. A water jacket around the furnace heats water.

Insulated lids

Flue

Hot plate for slow cooking

Hot plate for quick cooking

Baking and roasting oven

Slow-cooking oven

Thermostat

Water heating space

Coal stove

Fire grate

Fire unit

Heat insulation

35

Heating with Gas

Of all the kinds of central heating systems, gas central heating is the most convenient. You need no storage tanks or fuel store. The gas is piped directly to the furnace from the gas main.

When the furnace is operating, the gas flows from the inlet pipe through a control valve to the burners. There it is ignited and burns with a very hot flame. The hot gases rise and pass over coils of tubing through which water is circulating. The gases heat the tubing, which heats the water inside. The hot water is then pumped through the central heating system, passing through and heating up radiators in the rooms.

Like most other kinds of central heating furnaces, the gas supply is switched on by a time switch. This is a switch operated by a clock mechanism.

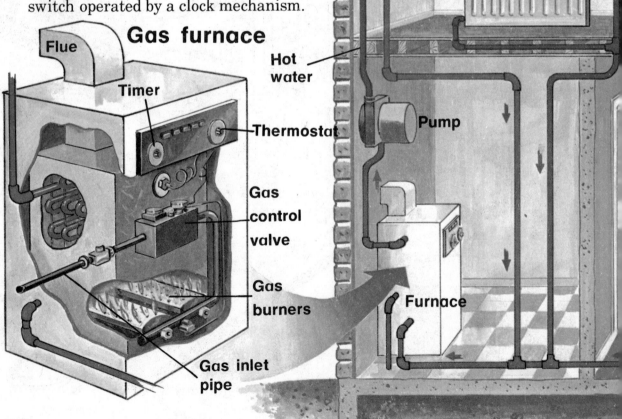

Air vent pipe

Expansion tank

First heating circuit

Panel radiator

Air valve

Hot water

Pump

Furnace

Gas furnace

Flue

Timer

Thermostat

Gas control valve

Gas burners

Gas inlet pipe

The time switch cuts in the pump and turns on the gas supply according to a built-in program, or set of instructions. These are selected by pushing a button or turning a dial. A thermostat, or heat switch, switches on the furnace when the water temperature drops and turns it off when the temperature reaches the desired level. A small flame, called the pilot, always burns in the boiler. This lights the main burners when the gas supply is turned on by the furnace thermostat or the time switch.

The furnace may also be switched on by a room thermostat, which responds to room temperature. Most room thermostats are worked by a bimetallic strip. This consists of two pieces of different metals joined together. When the temperature changes, the metals expand or contract by different amounts. This bends the strips, which makes or breaks an electrical contact to switch the furnace on or off.

Early central heating systems used wide, or large-bore pipes to carry the hot water from radiator to radiator. They relied on natural circulation to carry hot water through the pipes and radiators. In natural circulation the hot water rises because it is lighter, and the cold water sinks because it is heavier.

Most modern systems, however, use narrow, or small-bore copper pipes, and a pump is needed to pump the hot water through them.

The water circulates around and around the central heating system continually. Sometimes it overheats and expands and overflows into the expansion tank. When it cools, more water from the tank flows back into the system.

Second heating circuit

Hand control

Water return pipe

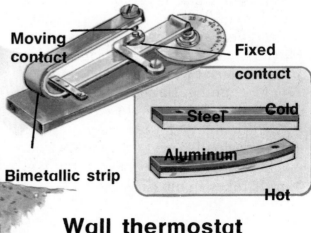

Moving contact

Fixed contact

Bimetallic strip

Steel Cold

Aluminum

Hot

Wall thermostat

Heating by Electricity

Electricity can also be used to run central heating systems. Since electricity is more expensive than other fuels, these systems generally cost more to operate. In England there is a plan to use electricity at times when most other users do not – for example, during the night and very early in the morning. At such times electricity is sold at a cheaper rate than normal. The drawback of "off-peak" systems is that heat is produced at a time when you don't want it, so these systems have to store the heat in some way.

In one form of electric central heating, heat is produced under the floors of the rooms. The heating elements are embedded in the concrete of the floors. They are plastic tubes containing wire coils that heat up when electricity passes through them.

The surrounding concrete absorbs the heat from the elements and gradually becomes hotter and hotter, and it keeps hot for a long time after the electricity is switched off. It thus acts to store heat. Beneath the concrete layer is a thick layer of insulation, which stops the heat going downwards.

Storage heaters work in a similar way. They contain blocks of concrete or other material which have heating elements running through them. They become very hot while the electricity is switched on, and then release their heat gradually over a long period. Some storage heaters have a built-in fan. It takes in air from the room and blows it past the heated blocks. This makes the heater give out its heat faster.

Both the underfloor and the storage heating systems are connected to a separate electrical circuit from the rest of the house. This circuit has its own meter and a time switch to ensure that the heating is used only during the "off-peak" periods.

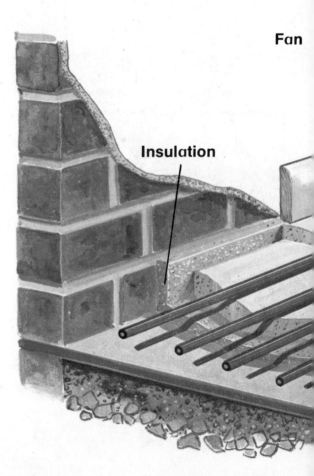

Fan

Insulation

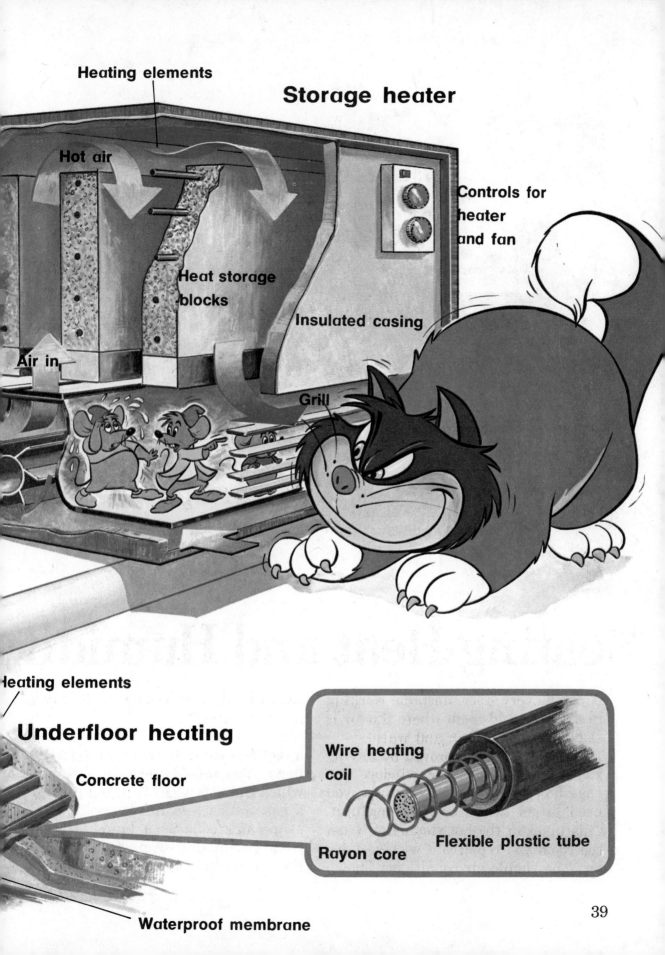

Heating elements

Storage heater

Hot air

Controls for heater and fan

Heat storage blocks

Insulated casing

Air in

Grill

Heating elements

Underfloor heating

Concrete floor

Wire heating coil

Rayon core

Flexible plastic tube

Waterproof membrane

39

Beating Heat and Humidity

It can be very uncomfortable working in a hot, humid room where the air is smelly, smoky, damp and warm.

Matters can be improved by having an exhaust fan in the window (see page 58), but for the best results you need to get an air-conditioning unit. This takes in the hot steamy air from the room and replaces it with cool dry air. The simple air conditioner shown

works in more or less the same way as a refrigerator.

It has pipes and coils through which a cooling substance called a refrigerant flows. The refrigerant is a substance which changes easily from a liquid into a gas and back again. It goes into the evaporator coils as a liquid. Hot air from inside the room is drawn over these coils by a fan. The coils absorb heat from the air, which goes back, cool, into the room.

As it absorbs heat, the liquid refrigerant in the evaporator coils changes into gas. The gas then passes into a compressor, which is driven by an electric motor. There it is compressed and becomes warm. It then passes through the condenser coils, over which outside air is blown by another fan. The hot refrigerant gas cools as it flows through the coils and condenses, or changes back into liquid. Then it passes back through the evaporator coils.

Some air conditioners have additional features, such as filters. Some filters remove dust and smoke particles from the air. Others remove smells. Most air conditioners have a drip pan fitted beneath the evaporator coils to collect any moisture that condenses as the air is cooled.

In many buildings air conditioning is carried out on a large scale from a central system. The air is circulated through a number of units. These units cool it or heat it as necessary; humidify or dehumidify it, and filter it.

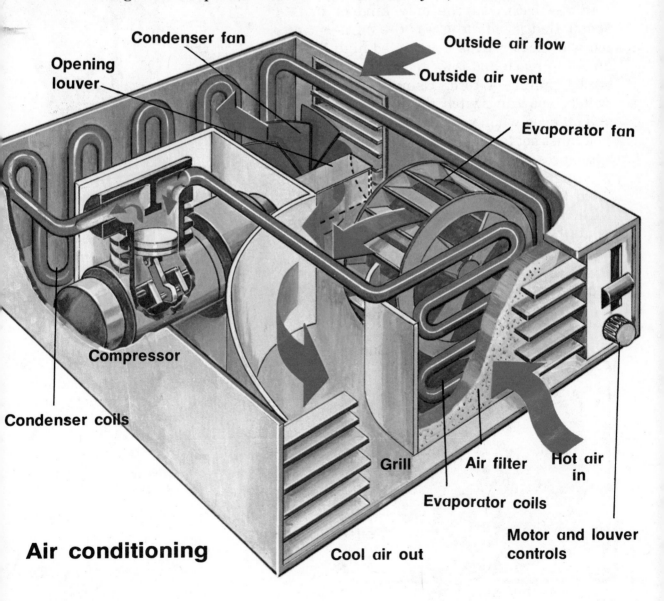

Condenser fan

Opening louver

Outside air flow

Outside air vent

Evaporator fan

Compressor

Condenser coils

Grill

Air filter

Hot air in

Evaporator coils

Motor and louver controls

Cool air out

Air conditioning

Space Heaters

Infrared heater

Radiant heat

Even in a centrally heated house there are some spaces in which you sometimes need extra warmth. For example, you may need it while you are having a bath. Heaters that provide extra warmth over a limited space are often called space heaters.

In the bathroom the only kind of heater that is safe to use is the infrared wall heater. This is mounted high up out of reach and is switched on and off by pulling a cord. Using a cord switch, you can switch the heater on and off even when your hands are wet. You must not touch electric switches or appliances with wet hands. If you do, you might get an electric shock which could kill you.

The infrared heater has a silica tube as its heating element. (Silica is the material that sand and flint are made

of.) The tube glows red hot, and the heat is thrown out by a polished metal reflector. A lot of heat comes out as invisible infrared waves, which gives the heater its name.

In other parts of the house other electric space heaters may be used. The

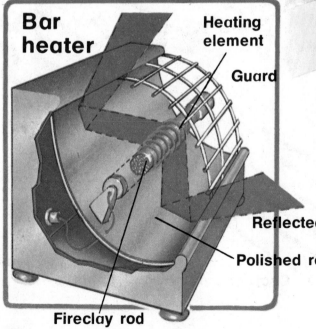

Bar heater

Heating element

Guard

Reflected heat

Polished reflector

Fireclay rod

42

Polished reflector

Guard

Coiled heater element

Silica tube

bar heater is a common one. This has one or two bars made of fireclay, around which the heating wire is coiled. The wire glows red hot when electricity passes through it. The heat is thrown out by a polished reflector.

Another popular space heater is the blow heater. In this heater a fan draws in cool air from the room and blows it over the hot heating elements. The air thus emerges warm. These heaters have controls to adjust the amount of heat coming from the elements and the speed of the air flowing over them.

In another common type of electric heater, the convector, warm air is allowed to flow upwards naturally from the heating coils. This has a heat switch, or thermostat, which switches it off when the desired temperature has been reached. The thermostat switches the heater back on whenever the temperature falls.

In some places it is illegal to use certain space heaters because they do not have safety features, making them dangerous to use.

Electric motor

Heater and fan controls

Fan

Air flow

Warm air out

Heating coil

Grill

Air inlet vents

Cool air in

Blow heater

Gas and Kerosene Heaters

Gas fires have been heating houses for over a hundred years. In the early days the gas was made from coal, but today most comes from the ground. It is called natural gas and burns with a very hot flame.

The fixed form of gas heater is connected to the gas main. It can be in a fireplace, and then hot fumes from the burning gas go through a flue into the chimney. The fire gives out heat in two ways.

First, the gas flames heat up an element made from fireclay (baked clay) and make it glow red hot. The element radiates heat into the room. Secondly, the fire heats up the air. Cold air passes into the fire through an inlet duct. It is heated by the hot fumes coming from the burning gas which pass around the duct. This arrangement is called a heat exchanger. The flue gases going out exchange heat with the cold air coming in.

Portable gas heaters use liquid gas for their fuel. This is gas that has been made liquid by pressure (squeezing). When you release the pressure, the liquid gas changes back into ordinary gas. Liquid gas is stored in strong steel cylinders. Like fixed gas fires, portable heaters both radiate heat and heat up the air. They have what is called a "balanced flue." This means that when the gas burns it produces no smelly or harmful fumes. Both portable heaters and modern fixed gas fires have auto-

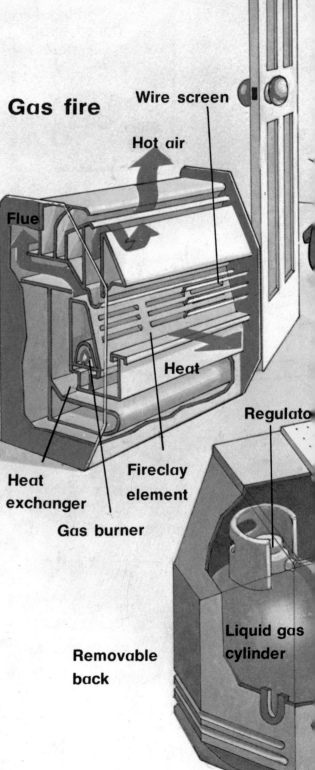

Gas fire

Wire screen

Hot air

Flue

Heat

Regulato

Heat exchanger

Fireclay element

Gas burner

Removable back

Liquid gas cylinder

Kerosene stove

Hot air

Chimney

Window

Burner wick

Wick control

Kerosene tank

Switch control

Gas inlet

Burner

Portable gas heater

matic ignition and light when they are switched on.

The paraffin heater shown here is a convector, which heats up the air. It has a wick made out of coarse woven material, which dips down into the paraffin and soaks it up. You light the wick with a match and then adjust the size of the flame by turning the wick control up or down. In this model the upper part is hinged. You lower it to light the wick.

Water Heaters

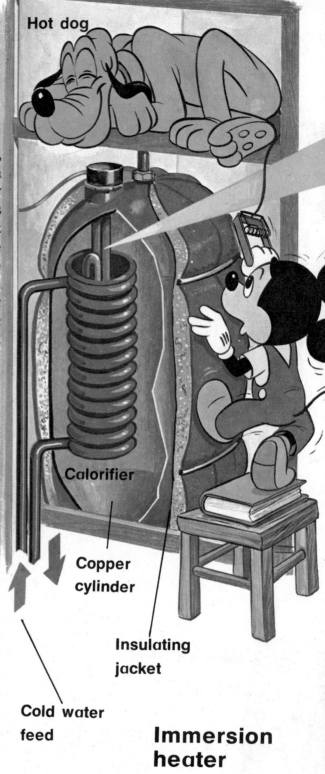

In houses which have central heating, hot water for washing and cleaning can be provided by the furnace. Pipes carry hot water from the boiler into coils inside a hot water cylinder. The heat from the water passing through the coils heats up the water inside the cylinder.

In summer, when the central heating furnace is turned off, an electric immersion heater can be used to heat water in the cylinder. This is so called because it is immersed in, or dips into the water.

The immersion heating element is much the same as the element in an electric kettle, but is much bigger. It consists of a metal tube which contains a heating coil embedded inside insulation.

At the top, where the immersion unit is screwed into the cylinder, there is a cover plate. Beneath it are the connections for the electrical supply. There is also a screw which you adjust to control the temperature of the water in the cylinder. It is connected to a thermostat, which switches off the electricity when the desired temperature is reached. The thermostat switches the electricity on again when the temperature of the hot water falls. To prevent the hot water cylinder losing too much heat to the air, it is covered with a thick insulating cover.

In houses connected to a gas main, the water may be heated in a different

Hot dog

Calorifier

Copper cylinder

Insulating jacket

Cold water feed

Immersion heater

Cover plate

Regulator screw

Electric lead

Pilot light

Casing

Burners

element

Insulation

Gas heater

Heating coil

Gas control

Temperature control

way. This water heater is mounted near where the water is needed. When you turn on the inlet control, the cold water flows past a valve and up through the heating coils. The pressure of the cold water flowing in turns on the gas supply to the burners. A tiny pilot light, which is always burning, lights all the burners. The burning gas rises and heats up the water flowing through the heating coils. The water flows from the outlet hot. When the heater is turned off, the water flow ceases and the gas supply to the burners stops. This heater only heats up as much water as you need, and is therefore very economical to run.

Insulation

Once you have heated your house you must try to keep the heat in. If you let too much of it escape, you will be throwing money away. There are several things you can do to insulate, or keep the heat in, your home.

As a start you can make sure the doors and windows fit properly. If they don't, hot air from inside can escape through the cracks, and cold drafts from outside can creep in. Outer doors need to have "weather stripping" to stop the rain beating in. A rubber pad at the bottom of the door will prevent drafts. Metal or foam strip can be fitted around the door frame to make it draft-proof.

Windows can be made draft-proof and insulated by double-glazing. This is done by putting in double panes of glass instead of single ones. The air

Double glazing

Air space

Airhole t
outside

Window sill

Draft excluder

Door

Weather ba

Rubber
insert

Weather trim

Outsid

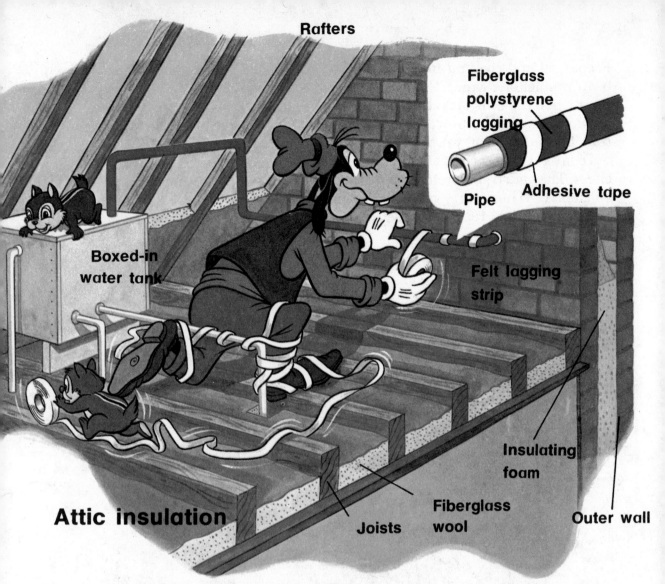

Fiberglass
polystyrene
lagging

Pipe

Adhesive tape

Boxed-in
water tank

Felt lagging
strip

Insulating
foam

Attic insulation

Joists

Fiberglass
wool

Outer wall

gap between the two panes of glass stops the heat from the inside pane getting to the outside.

Another very good way of insulating your house is to fill the cavity (hole) between the inner and outer walls with a plastic foam. The foam is pumped into the cavity as a liquid froth. It sets as a solid foam later. The foam can be put in a new house before the roof is put on. It can be put in an existing house through holes drilled in the walls. To complete the insulation of your house you must insulate the roof, or rather the loft. You do this by laying

fiberglass "wool" between the wooden beams or joists.

By preventing the heat rising into the loft you create a problem. In the loft are all the water tanks and lots of pipes for the central heating and water supply systems. If the water in them freezes, they will burst. Water will pour out into the house and cause a great deal of damage. To prevent this happening the pipes must also be insulated, or lagged. This is done with strips of felt or plastic foam. The water tanks can be boxed in with wooden boards or covered in a foam quilt.

Preparing and cooking food has never been simpler or cleaner. Gone are those days when the cook slaved for hours in a steamy atmosphere over a hot stove that burned coal or wood.

Today's stoves are neat and easy to clean. They burn gas or electricity most efficiently. These are much cleaner fuels, which are ready for use at the flick of a switch.

Electricity is put to use in many other ways in the kitchen. It boils kettles, percolates coffee, runs refrigerators and deep-freezes, and powers food mixers. Mixers are a great help in preparing food. Some can grind, liquidize, blend, chop and peel, as well as mix food.

Preparing Food

Mixing and Grinding

Preparing food can take quite a long time if you are using only your hands and a knife or fork. Mixing the ingredients for a cake takes ages and makes your wrist ache. Chopping up meat is tedious and can be dangerous if your fingers get in the way!

You can, however, avoid wrist-ache and cut fingers by taking advantage of the many machines and gadgets devised for use in the kitchen. One of the oldest is the grinder, which shreds up meat and other things. You feed the meat into the top, using a pusher to press it down. When you turn the handle, the feed screw moves the meat forward. The meat is shredded as it is forced through the holes of a fixed shear plate, and at the same time it is cut by a rotating knife edge which is attached to the end of the feed screw.

The mechanical chopper is also a useful tool, for chopping up vegetables such as carrots and onions. Pressing the handle forces the corrugated steel knife blade down through a guide. The spring makes it come back again. A simple ratchet device turns the knife blades around each time you chop.

Today many gadgets operate with the help of the electric motor. This powers mixers, blenders and grinders. In mixers the beaters are driven through right-angled gears, while in blenders and grinders the cutting blades are driven directly. Some processors can be fitted with all kinds of attachments, which allow them not only to mix, liquidize and grind but also to peel, mince, beat, chop and blend.

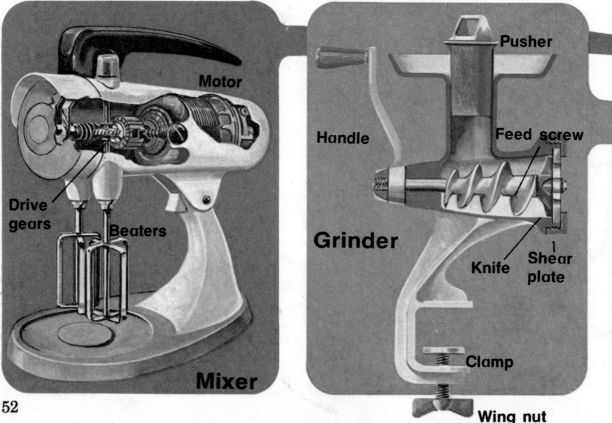

Mixer — Motor, Drive gears, Beaters

Grinder — Pusher, Handle, Feed screw, Knife, Shear plate, Clamp, Wing nut

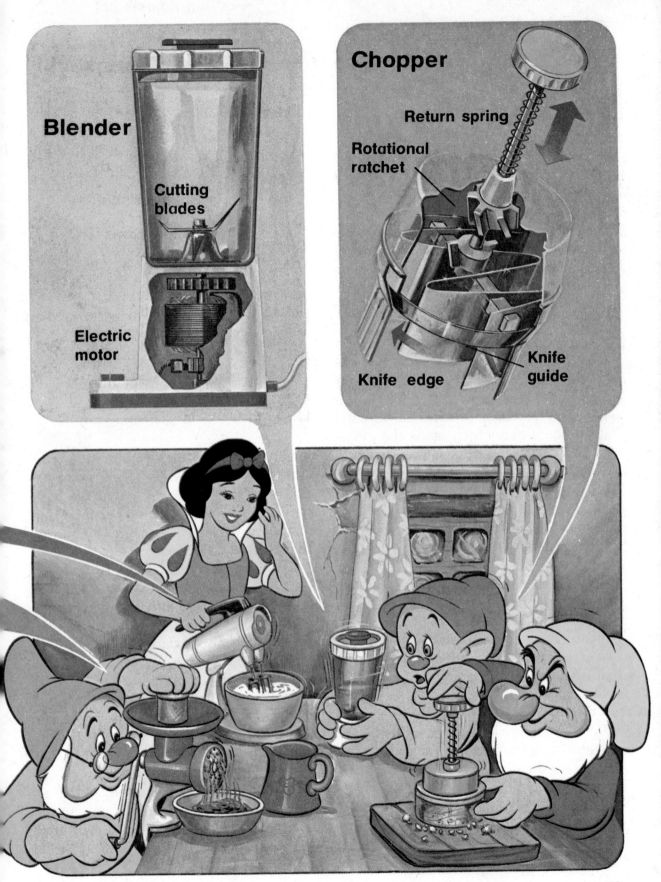

Blender

Cutting blades

Electric motor

Chopper

Return spring

Rotational ratchet

Knife edge

Knife guide

Weighing and Beating

Being a good cook is rather like being a good chemist. To get the best results you have to measure the ingredients carefully according to the recipe you are using. If you add too much of one thing and too little of another, then your dish may be ruined.

A good cook must keep handy a measuring cup to measure the volume of liquid ingredients, and a scale to measure the weight of solid ingredients. The common kind of kitchen scale has a pan which holds the material to be weighed. The shaft carrying the pan is attached by pivoted parallel arms to the body of the scale. A spring connects the lower arms to an adjustable screw on the top of the scale. A pointer is also attached to the lower arms.

When there is no weight in the pan, the spring pulls up the lower arms, and the pointer indicates zero on the scale. When weight is added, the spring stretches, the lower arms drop, and the pointer moves down the scale to indicate the weight.

When you have carefully measured the ingredients into a bowl, you will often have to mix them until they blend together. You can do this with a fork, but it is easier and quicker with a beater. The beater handle turns a large wheel called the crown wheel, which has teeth cut in both sides. These teeth

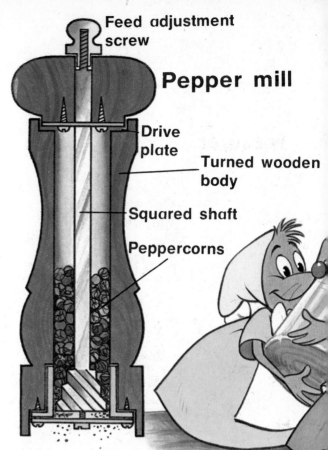

Pepper mill

Feed adjustment screw

Drive plate

Turned wooden body

Squared shaft

Peppercorns

mesh with and turn other toothed wheels, called pinions. The pinions are attached to shafts that carry the beaters. Because they are on opposite sides of the crown wheel, the pinions rotate in different directions.

Most recipes usually include the phrase "add seasoning to taste." By seasoning we mean salt and pepper and other spices. The best way of adding pepper is freshly ground from a pepper mill. The pepper mill contains metal plates which grind peppercorns into powder.

It is as well to concentrate when you are adding seasoning because if you add too much, that is the end of your meal, and you may be forced to resort to a can. Food from a can may not be as good, but at least you can prepare it quickly. Simply open the can, heat and serve.

Wall can opener

Cutter

Tension spring

Locking lever

Drive crank

Spur wheel

Pinion

Double crown drive wheel

Pan

Correction screw

Beater

Balance spring

Scale

Parallel arms

Kitchen scales

Boiling and Toasting

For many of us breakfast can be a hurried meal. Sometimes we scarcely have time to snatch a slice of toast and wash it down with milk, tea or coffee. When we are in a hurry, the electric kettle and toaster are a great help. The kettle can boil water and the toaster can brown toast in just a few minutes.

The water in an electric kettle is heated by an element. This is a metal tube containing a heating coil like that of an electric furnace. The ends of the element are fixed in an insulated unit, which fits through a hole in the kettle. A screw sleeve on the outside holds the unit tightly in place. Fiber washers on both sides of the hole prevent any water getting out. Contact pins project from the unit inside the sleeve. An electric plug fits over the pins to carry current to the heating coil. There is also another pin, which is

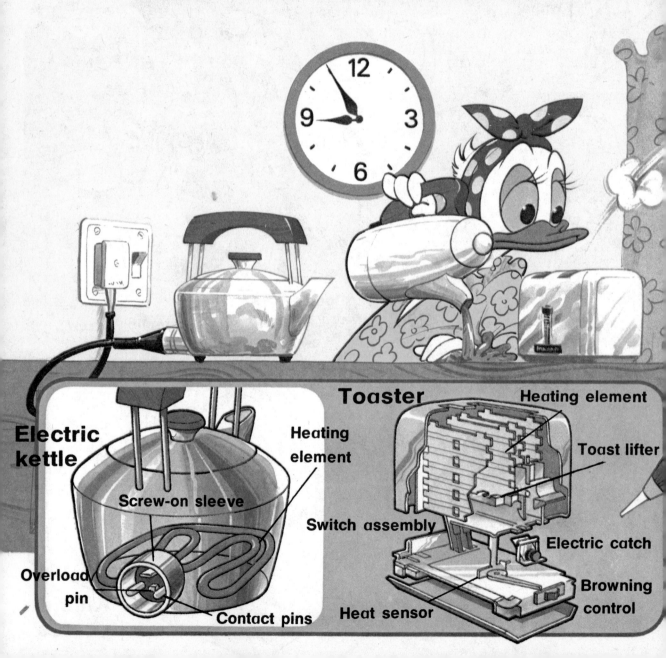

Electric kettle

Overload pin

Screw-on sleeve

Heating element

Contact pins

Toaster

Heating element

Toast lifter

Switch assembly

Electric catch

Heat sensor

Browning control

normally pushed in. If the kettle over-heats (overloads) this pin comes out and knocks out the plug.

The electric toaster has heating elements that you can see glowing. You switch them on when you push down the toast lifter. The heat from the elements browns the toast. When the toast is done, the temperature inside the toaster rises rapidly. This causes a kind of thermostat, or heat switch, to turn off the electricity. An electric catch then opens and allows the toast lifter to rise, and the toast to "pop up."

The quickest way to make coffee is to pour hot water on to "instant" coffee, but you make better tasting coffee in a percolator. In an electric percolator, the measured water is boiled by a heating element. The boiling water rises through a tube up to the lid. It falls back into a perforated (holed) basket containing freshly ground coffee beans. It trickles, or percolates, through the ground coffee and out through the holes in the basket. As it does so, the delicious flavor from the coffee beans goes into the water.

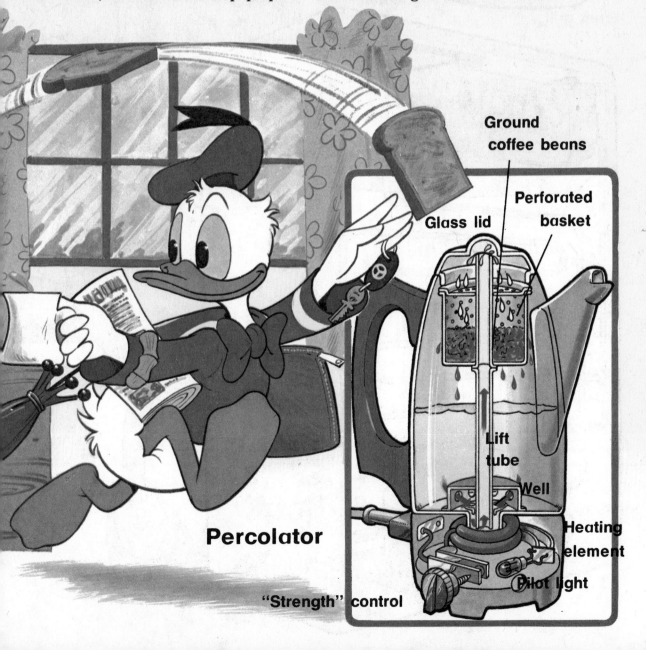

Ground coffee beans

Perforated basket

Glass lid

Percolator

Lift tube

Well

Heating element

Pilot light

"Strength" control

Exhaust fan

Switch unit

Backplate

Outer grill

Fan

Switch cord

Electric
motor

Refrigerator

Front grill

Evaporator coils

Freezer
compartment

Cold tray

Condenser coils

Motor

Compressor

58

Keeping Cool

When you are cooking a meal, the kitchen can become very hot and steamy. The heat from the stove and the steam from boiling saucepans make you feel very uncomfortable. A good way to keep cool is to fit an exhaust fan into the walls or windows. This sucks out the hot steamy air. Cooler fresh air from outside the kitchen moves in to take its place.

The fan shown here is a window unit. It is mounted inside a hole cut in the glass. The fan blades are driven by an electric motor. It is switched on and off by a cord.

Some foods can be harmed by the heat in the kitchen too, particularly perishable foods like milk and meat. To prevent these foods "going bad," or spoiling, they should be kept in a refrigerator, or fridge. There they are kept very cool.

In a refrigerator a liquid is made to evaporate, or change into vapor (gas). As it does so, it takes in heat from the food.

In the refrigerator the liquid evaporates inside coils around the freezing compartment. The vapor formed is then drawn into a compressor, where it is compressed (squeezed). It becomes hot as a result. It loses this heat when it passes through the coils of the condenser and changes into liquid again. The liquid then passes back through a valve into the evaporator coils, and the process begins again.

Electric Cooking

Cooking a meal has never been easier than it is today. The modern stoves we use heat up our pots and pans quickly and can easily be controlled. They may also be fitted with automatic timers that switch the heat on and off while we are doing something else.

Electricity is very clean to cook with. The picture shows an electric stove. It has four burners in the top, or hob unit, a grill and an oven. These burners are made up of spiral radiant elements. They are so called because they glow, or radiate heat. They contain coils which heat up when electricity passes through them.

Another radiant element forms the grill. In this stove the grill is located beneath the hob. In other stoves it can be mounted differently. Similar elements provide the heat for the oven. They are mounted at the sides behind removable linings. The outer walls of the oven are filled with insulation, such as fiberglass, to prevent the oven heat from escaping.

The oven has a double door. The inner glass door enables you to see how the cooking is progressing, without letting the heat out. The oven also has a light which goes on when you open the outer door. It is operated by a little push switch. Another thing you find in the oven is a thin rod. This is a thermometer, which takes the temperature of the oven.

You use dials on the control panel to switch on the various heating elements and to select the amount of heat you want. The dial for the oven is marked in temperature – the number of degrees centigrade (C) or Fahrenheit (F). When the oven is first switched on, a warning light glows on the panel. When the thermometer in the oven senses that the correct temperature has been reached, a thermostat (heat switch) turns the heat off. The warning light goes out. From then on the thermostat switches the heat on and off as necessary to keep the oven temperature constant.

If you want to get rid of cooking smells, you could add a hood. This has powerful fans which suck in the greasy, smelly air. The air passes first through a filter, which removes the grease. It then goes through a bed of charcoal, which removes the smells. When the air is blown back into the room from the hood, it is clean.

Hood

Clean air

Fans

Fluorescent light

Pilot light

Charcoal filter

Power switch

Control panel

Timer

Grill element

Oven light

Thermometer

Oven door

Inner glass door

Oven elements

Storage drawer

Light switch

Insulation

Electric stove

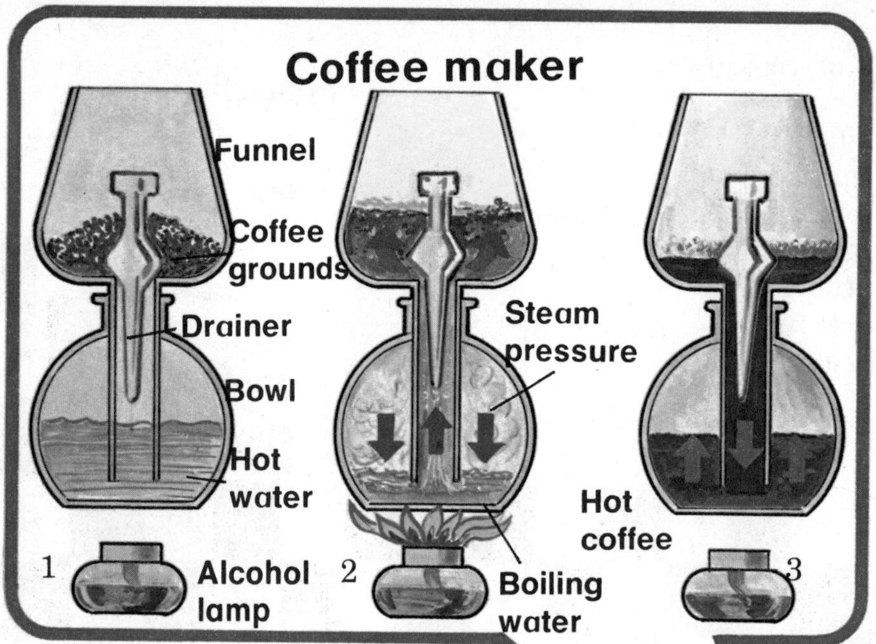

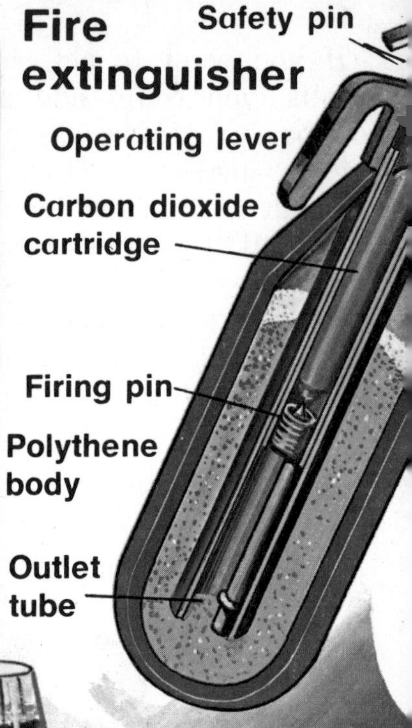

Coffee maker

Funnel

Coffee grounds

Drainer

Bowl

Hot water

Steam pressure

Hot coffee

1

2

3

Alcohol lamp

Boiling water

Fire extinguisher

Safety pin

Operating lever

Carbon dioxide cartridge

Firing pin

Polythene body

Outlet tube

Cooking with Gas

Many people cook with gas rather than with electricity. On a gas stove the level of heat can be very easily controlled. For example, heat is available from a burner the instant the gas is turned on. There is no "warm-up" period as there is with an electric burner. Also, with gas, the heating ceases as soon as the gas is turned off.

One disadvantage the gas stove has, however, is that it gives out more fumes than an electric stove. They come from the burning gas. So it is advisable to have a hood fitted over a gas stove.

You had to light the burners on early gas stoves with a match or with a battery lighter. The battery made a thin wire glow, which ignited the gas. Some gas stoves have an electrical ignition system built into each burner.

In most places these days the gas used for cooking is natural gas. This is gas taken from the ground. It has replaced town gas, which was made mainly from coal. In the gas burner the gas mixes with air to form an inflammable mixture. This burns with a very hot flame when it is ignited, and the heat from the flames does the cooking. The grill, however, works in a different way. First the grill burner flames heat up a metal mesh, or fret, to red heat. Then the fret radiates heat to grill toast and meat.

Gas stove

Nozzle

Grill

Ignition electrode

Grill burner

Timing dials

Burner fret

Ignition button

Burner head

Flue

Heat flow

Oven burner

Storage compartment

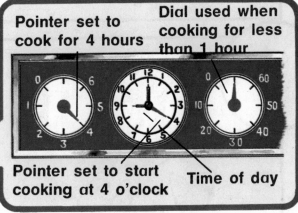

Pointer set to cook for 4 hours

Dial used when cooking for less than 1 hour

Pointer set to start cooking at 4 o'clock

Time of day

The coffee maker shown here is made of heat-resistant glass. It works by pressure in the following way:

1. Hot water is placed in the bowl; ground coffee in the funnel.

2. An alcohol lamp heats the water in the bowl to boiling point. The steam produced forces the boiling water up through the funnel. There it extracts the flavor.

3. The alcohol lamp is put out, and the steam in the bowl cools. This sets up a partial vacuum, which sucks the coffee back through the funnel.

For safety's sake it is a good idea to keep a fire extinguisher handy in the kitchen. Then you can put out small fires before they grow into big ones. This extinguisher sprays carbon dioxide gas which replaces the air around the burning material. With no air available, the material stops burning.

63

Microwave oven

Pressure cooker

Time selector

On/off switch

Clamp-down lid

Weighted safety valve

Power selection switch

Saucepan

Speedy Cooking

On modern electric and gas stoves cooking is much quicker than it used to be, but using ordinary pots and pans, it can still take a long time.

Modern science, however, has come to the aid of the cook and produced devices that can cook food in a fraction of the normal time. One is the pressure cooker; the other is the microwave oven.

The pictures show a speedy cooking contest. Three meals are started at the same time using, from left to right, a microwave oven, a pressure cooker, and an ordinary saucepan to heat the food. Within just a few minutes the food in the microwave oven is ready. The pressure cooker takes somewhat longer; but even after two hours the food in the saucepan is still not ready!

In ordinary saucepan cooking, the heat from the stove heats the pan. The pan heats the water, and the water heats the food. Heat passes slowly from the outside to the inside of the food. In ordinary cooking the water cannot get any hotter than boiling point (212° F).

In pressure cooking, water is made to boil under pressure. When it does so, it boils at a higher temperature. It therefore cooks food faster. A microwave oven heats food in a totally different way. It bombards the food with invisible radio waves called microwaves. These get right inside the food and make all its tiny molecules vibrate rapidly which cause the food to heat up.

Cleaning

Keeping the home spick and span was once an endless task for the housewife, who spent most of the day "tied to the kitchen sink." Today she has all kinds of machines to help her with the household chores.

Washing is no longer a drudgery. Washing machines make light work of washing clothes; some operate automatically. Dishwashers swiftly dispose of washing and drying, preventing sore hands – and dropped plates! Even cleaning your teeth is less of a chore than it was, when you use an electric toothbrush.

Vacuum cleaners, sweepers and shampooers help keep floors and carpets dust free and bright. They are easy and speedy to use, not controlled by magic, but by electricity.

The Vacuum Cleaner

Carpets help keep our homes cosy and warm, but they do pick up a lot of dirt and dust. It is very hard to remove the dirt by hand, but easy when you have a vacuum cleaner.

The vacuum cleaner sucks air through the carpet fibers, and the air carries with it the bits of dirt and dust. The picture shows a cylinder vacuum cleaner, which works by suction alone. The suction is produced by an extractor fan, which is spun by an electric motor. Air is sucked into the cleaner through a tube and flexible hose. It passes first into a bag, where it deposits the dirt it carries. It is sucked into the fan and then blown out through the outlet. The hose can also be fitted into the outlet so that the cleaner can be used to blow dirt away.

The other main type of vacuum cleaner stands upright and has a handle. Air is sucked by a fan through a hole in the bottom of the cleaner body. A rotating roller brushes and beats the carpet to free the dust. The roller is driven by a rubber band from a spindle on the fan. The dust is collected in a bag attached to the handle.

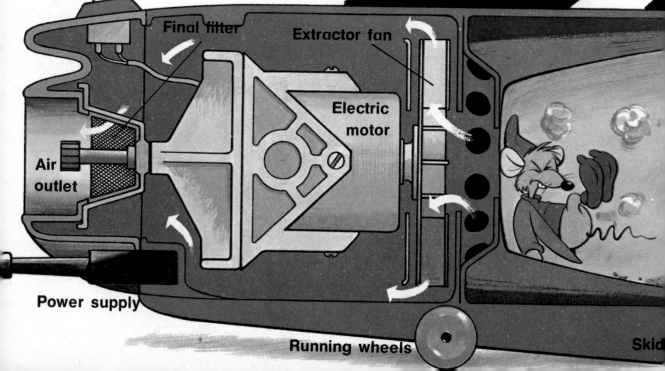

On/off switch

Final filter

Extractor fan

Electric motor

Air outlet

Power supply

Running wheels

Skid

Flexible hose

Removable dust bag

Suction fitting

Carpet Care

You do not have to use a vacuum cleaner to clean the carpets. There are good sweepers available that you simply push over the carpet to clean it. They have four wheels with rubber-band tires. As the wheels go round, the tires make contact with and turn a roller brush.

As it turns, the brush sweeps the dirt from the carpet into the two dustpans. The dustpans are hinged on one side and can be sprung open for emptying. You move a lever on top of the sweeper body to do this.

Some of the latest carpet sweepers have a built-in comb to clean the bristles, preventing them from becoming tangled with hair and cotton. Some

Carpet sweeper

Handle

Bail

Synthetic bristles

Brush roller

Dustpans

Spring

Rubber sweeper tires

Shampooer

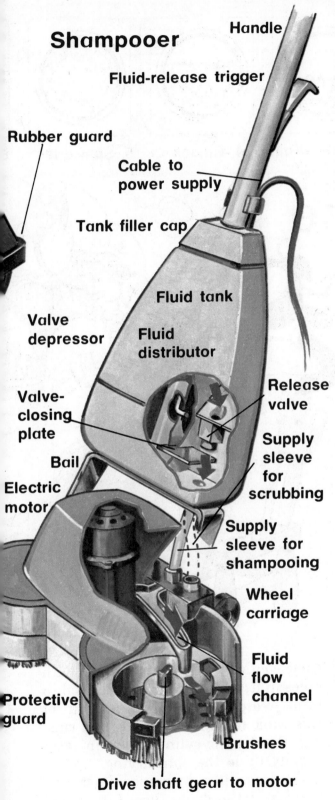

Handle

Fluid-release trigger

Rubber guard

Cable to power supply

Tank filler cap

Fluid tank

Valve depressor

Fluid distributor

Release valve

Valve-closing plate

Supply sleeve for scrubbing

Bail

Electric motor

Supply sleeve for shampooing

Wheel carriage

Fluid flow channel

Protective guard

Brushes

Drive shaft gear to motor

also have rotating brushes in the front corners to dislodge dirt close to the walls or around furniture legs. They may also have a device for adjusting the height of the roller brush for carpets with piles of different depths.

However carefully you sweep the carpet, sooner or later it will become so dirty that you will need to shampoo it. If you have many four-legged friends, it will be sooner rather than later!

Shampooing the carpet by hand is a long and backbreaking job. So it is best to borrow, buy or hire a carpet shampooer. The one shown here not only shampoos carpets, it can also be used with different brushes and pads to scrub, wax and polish other kinds of floor coverings such as vinyl, tile and woodblock.

In the carpet shampooer the water and shampoo solution is poured into a tank attached to the handle. At the top of the handle is a trigger mechanism which operates a valve at the bottom of the tank. When you pull the trigger, the valve opens and allows shampoo solution to travel down the pipe, or supply sleeve, which connects with the base of the shampooer.

In the base are two circular brushes which are spun round by an electric motor. The discs carrying the brushes have holes in them. The shampoo solution from the supply sleeve goes into a T-shaped distributing channel and falls on to the discs. It drops on to the carpet through the holes, and the rotating brushes rub it in thoroughly.

The shampoo makes the carpet fibers release the dirt on them. When the carpet is dry, it can then be vacuum cleaned. The loosened dirt is removed, leaving a beautifully clean carpet.

Operating cycle

1. Pre-soaks **2. Washes** **3. Water drains** **4. Rinses** **5. Spin dries** 6

Washing, the Easy Way

Once we used to wash clothes in soap and water, rubbing them together with our hands to remove the dirt.

Doing washing these days is a lot easier. The hard work is done by machines, and detergents are used which wash better than ordinary soaps.

There are two main types of washing machines – the twin-tub machine and the drum, or cylinder machine. In the twin-tub machine, washing and spin drying take place in separate units. The washing tub is filled with water from the tap by hand. It is brought to the right temperature by a heater. Then the clothes are put in, and the machine is switched on. An electric motor turns a paddle wheel, or agitator, to keep the clothes moving.

After washing, the clothes are transferred to the separate spin dryer. This is a cylinder with holes in it, which is spun rapidly around by another motor. Water is flung out from the clothes and escapes through the holes.

In the drum-type machine, washing, rinsing and spinning take place in the same container. This is a cylinder with holes in it, which spins around inside a tank. Water is pumped in and out of this tank to do the washing and rinsing. Finally the cylinder is spun extra rapidly to do the spin drying.

The washing machine illustrated here is of the drum type. Like many drum machines it works automatically.

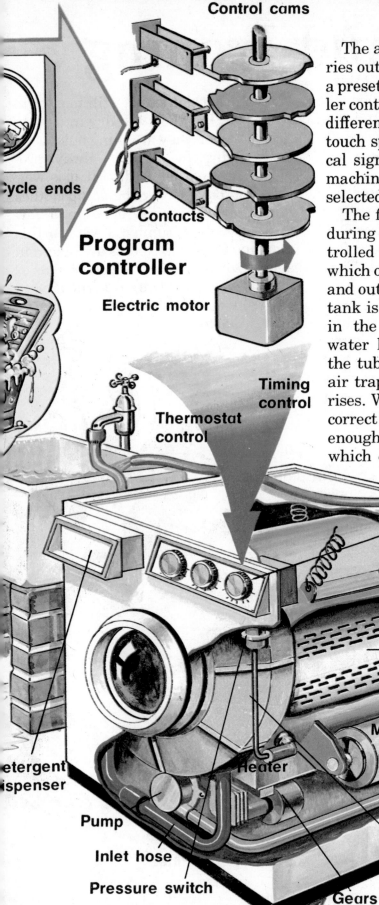

Control cams

Cycle ends

Contacts

Program controller

Electric motor

The automatic washing machine carries out its operating cycle according to a preset program. The program controller contains a series of cams, or discs, of different shapes. As they turn, they touch spring contacts and send electrical signals to the various parts of the machine. Different programs can be selected to suit different fabrics.

The filling and emptying of the tank during washing and rinsing are controlled by means of electrical signals which open and close valves in the inlet and outlet pipes. The water level in the tank is controlled by a pressure switch in the water level tube. When the water level in the tank rises, that in the tube rises too. The pressure of the air trapped in the top of the tube also rises. When the water has reached the correct level, the air pressure is high enough to operate the pressure switch which closes the water valve.

Timing control

Thermostat control

Program selector

Spin drying and washing drum

Drive belt

Motor

Automatic washing machine

Detergent dispenser

Heater

Pump

Inlet hose

Pressure switch

Gears

Water level tube

Outlet hose

73

Drying and Ironing

After clothes have been washed and rinsed, they have to be dried and then ironed. Ironing smooths out the wrinkles in the clothes, making them look neat once more.

In the old days, excess water was removed from washed clothes by a mangle. The dripping wet clothes were forced between the mangle rollers which squeezed out the water. Some modern washing machines are fitted with mangles, now operated electrically, not by hand. Other washing machines have spin dryers, which spin the wet clothes around at very high speed – 3,000 times a minute or more. The water is flung outward by centrifugal force, leaving the clothes much drier.

Spin-dried clothes are still too wet to be ironed, but they will dry in next to no time when they are hung outside on the washing line. That is, always provided the weather is dry. If it is wet, then you have to dry the damp clothes indoors. This can be done in a few minutes with a tumble dryer. In this machine the damp clothes are placed in a large drum, which is perforated, or has holes in. The drum is turned round and round by a drive belt from an electric motor.

Tumble dryer

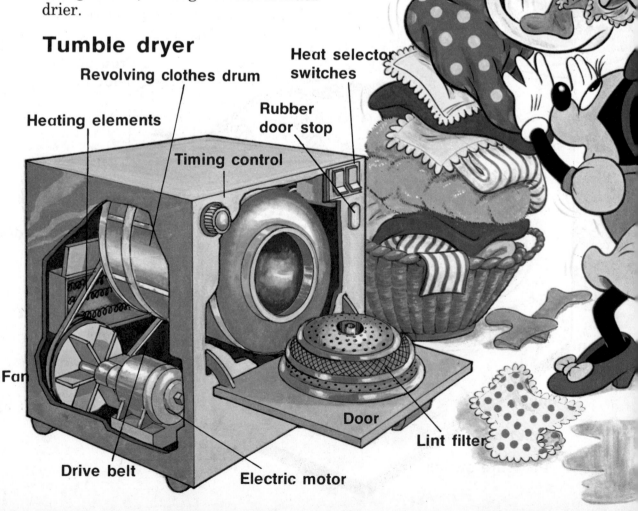

Revolving clothes drum

Heat selector switches

Heating elements

Rubber door stop

Timing control

Fan

Drive belt

Electric motor

Door

Lint filter

The motor also drives a fan, which blows air over a set of heating coils, or elements. The warm air coming out goes through the holes into the drum. The clothes are dried as they tumble around in the warm air. The moist air leaves the front of the drum through a filter, which collects the lint, or fluff from the clothes. You can vary the time and temperature of drying by setting dials. If you are going to iron the tumble-dried clothes afterwards, you need not have them bone dry. They iron better if they are slightly damp.

Early irons were literally slabs of iron with a handle that were heated by the fire. Today's irons are electric. They have an element which heats up when electricity is passed through it. It passes on its heat to the sole plate, or flat bottom of the iron. You can control the temperature of the iron by means of a dial. This works a thermostat, which switches the electricity on or off in order to maintain the required temperature.

Most modern irons are steam irons. They contain small tanks which can be filled with water. When the steam control is "on," a valve at the bottom of the tank opens and allows water to drip onto the element. It immediately turns into steam and fills the steam chamber. It escapes through vents in the sole plate and passes into the clothes being ironed. Steam ironing is necessary for ironing very dry clothes and for pressing creases and pleats.

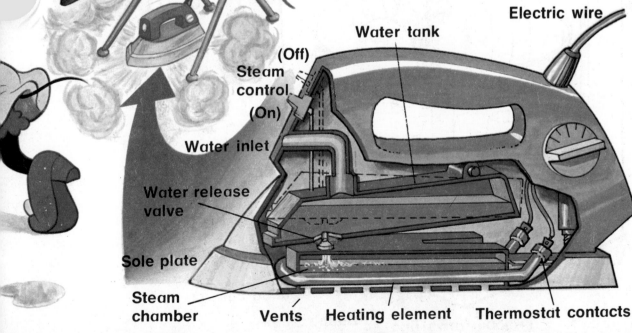

Steam iron

Electric wire

Water tank

(Off)
Steam control
(On)

Water inlet

Water release valve

Sole plate

Steam chamber

Vents   Heating element   Thermostat contacts

Washing Up

Perhaps one of the most thankless tasks of the housewife, her husband or her children, is doing the dishes. Washing piles of dirty dishes and greasy pans is no fun. You can end up with sore hands and, if you are not careful, broken plates!

If you dread the washing-up, an automatic dishwasher is the answer. You just pack in the dirty cups, plates, dishes and cutlery and switch on. You can forget about washing up and retire to your armchair. In an hour or less, everything that was dirty and greasy will be sparkling clean and dry, ready to be put away in the cupboard.

In most dishwashers you stack the plates, cups, and so on, in plastic-covered trays. To begin with you fill the soap dispensers properly. A heater in the bottom of the machine heats water to the right temperature. The hot water is pumped through two rotating spray arms, or rotors, at top and bot-

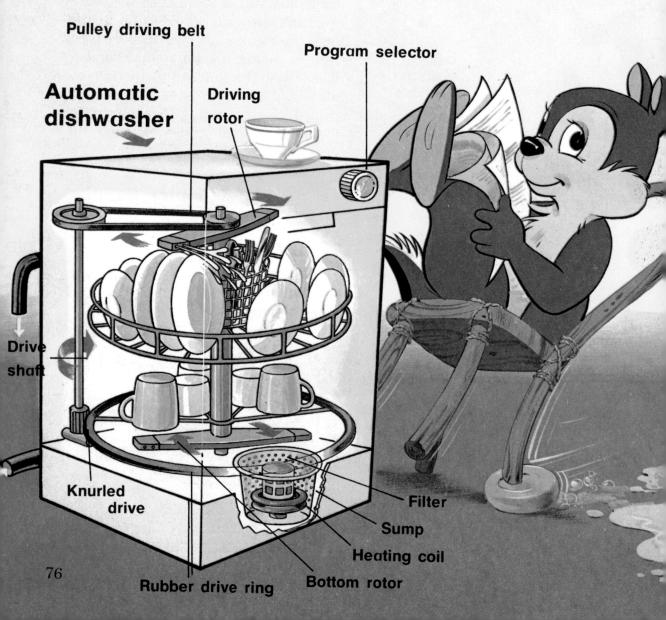

Pulley driving belt

Program selector

Automatic dishwasher

Driving rotor

Drive shaft

Knurled drive

Filter

Sump

Heating coil

Rubber drive ring

Bottom rotor

tom. It emerges from the spray arms as powerful jets which penetrate every nook and cranny of the wash load, removing all dirt and grease. Many machines contain a water softener to help the cleaning operation.

As with a washing machine, you can select a washing program to suit the items you want to wash. The machine will then go through a sequence of prewashing, washing and rinsing in warm or hot water. There are different settings for delicate washing for fine glassware or tough washing for dirty pans. At the end of the wash cycle, a pump automatically drains the water from the machine, allowing the now clean utensils inside to dry.

There is usually a perforated container at the bottom of the machine, which traps any scraps that were left on the dirty plates.

Manual dishwasher

Shaver outlet

Bathroom scale

Calibrating spring

Receiving lever

78

Electric shavers

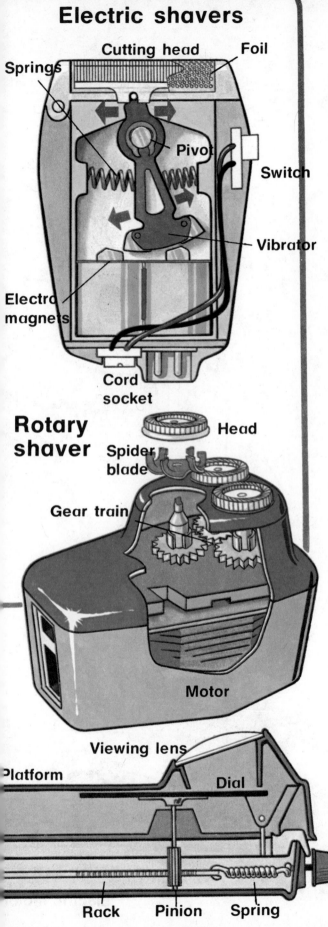

Cutting head

Foil

Springs

Pivot

Switch

Vibrator

Electro magnets

Cord socket

Rotary shaver

Head

Spider blade

Gear train

Motor

Viewing lens

Platform

Dial

Rack   **Pinion**   **Spring**

Zero adjusting knob

A Close Shave

Although many men still shave with razor blades, others prefer to use an electric razor.

The commonest kind of electric shaver has a many bladed cutting head, which moves rapidly back and forth beneath a piece of thin foil. In shaving, the whiskers are sheared off as they poke through the holes of the foil. The cutting head is mounted on an arm with a piece of iron on the end – the armature. The armature is attracted first one way and then the other by the electromagnets, making the cutting head move back and forth.

Another kind of electric shaver has rotating cutting heads. They are driven by gears from an electric motor.

Weight for It!

Another useful thing to have in the bathroom is a scale. The usual scale has an arrangement of springs and levers to measure the weight upon it. When someone stands on the platform, their weight is transmitted by a ridge and receiving lever to a thick calibrating spring. The spring stretches more or less according to the weight of the person on the scale.

The movement of this spring moves the crank and the toothed rack attached to it. As the rack moves, it turns around a toothed gearwheel, or pinion. On top of this pinion is the dial which has weights marked on it. A magnifying lens above the dial makes it easier to read.

79

Hair Care

Most people try to be glamorous; and what a lot of time you can spend washing and combing your hair.

Hair can indeed take a long time to dry after it has been washed, but drying can be speeded up by using a hair dryer, which works by electricity. The electricity turns a fan and heats up a coil, or heating element. The fan sucks in cold air from the room and blows it past the heating element.

You can direct the stream of hot air on to your hair by holding the hair dryer close to it, or you can use the hose and bag attachment.

If you want to keep your hair looking neat and in place, you can spray it with lacquer. The lacquer holds it in position. The spray comes from what is called an aerosol can. Inside the can the lacquer is dissolved in a liquid which is under pressure. This liquid is called the propellant. When the release button of the can is pressed, the pressure inside the can propels the liquid out through a nozzle as a fine spray. In the air the propellant evaporates, or turns to gas, leaving the lacquer as a mist of tiny droplets.

When you gaze in the mirror you don't see yourself exactly as other people see you. You see a "mirror image" of yourself. Your right eye appears to be your left eye in the mirror; your left hand appears to be your right hand; and so on. Reflection does not take place in the glass, of course, because glass is transparent – you can see through it. Reflection takes place in a very thin coating of silver on the back of the glass.

Heating element

Heat control

Electric motor

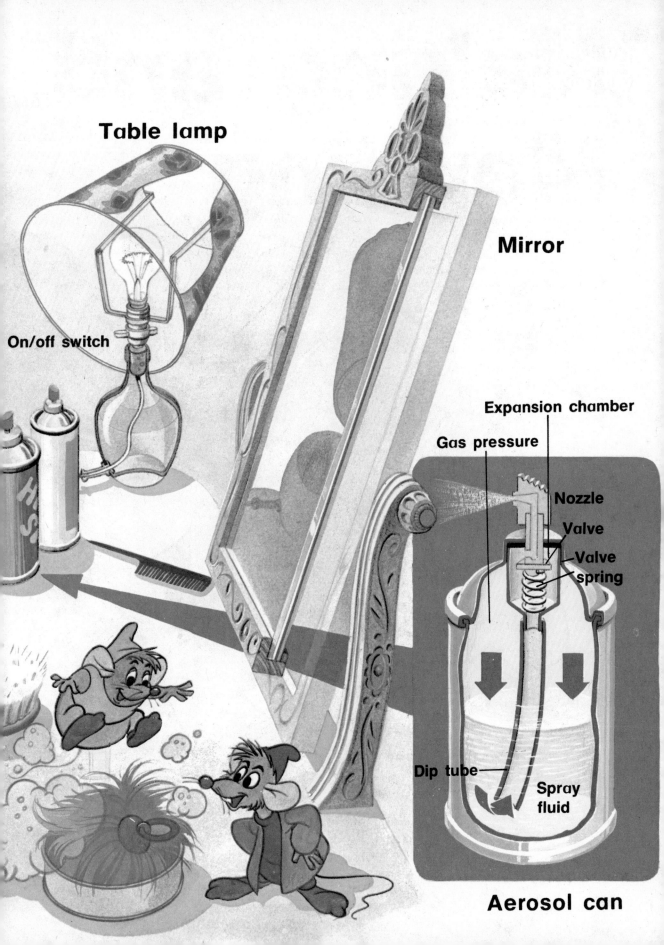

Table lamp

On/off switch

Mirror

Expansion chamber

Gas pressure

Nozzle

Valve

Valve spring

Dip tube

Spray fluid

Aerosol can

Making and Mending

People began wearing clothes many thousands of years ago. At first they simply draped the skins of animals around their bodies. Then they learned to sew, and sewed skins together into better fitting garments. The needle was one of the first tools early man invented. About 10,000 years ago he learned how to spin fibers into thread and weave thread into cloth.

Things have not really changed fundamentally since then. Spinning and weaving are still the main ways of making fabrics, and the needle is still one of the housewife's best friends.

Knitting and Weaving

Many people knit and weave by machine at home.

The knitting machine shown below works with what are called latch needles. They have a hook at the end with a tiny latch fitted which makes the hook into an "eye" when it is closed. Then the thread, or yarn, is fed to a carriage which the knitter moves from side to side to make a row of knitting.

As the carriage moves, it carries the yarn across each needle in turn. It also causes the needles to move back and forth in such a way as to form a stitch. The inset diagram at the top shows how a stitch is made:

1. The needle moves forward, and the previous stitch, or loop, pushes the latch open.

2. The loop slips behind the open latch.

3. The needle moves back and the loop knocks the latch shut.

4. The loop slips off the needle, which draws yarn through it to form a new loop, or stitch.

Different patterns are made in the knitwear by feeding instructions into the machine in the form of a punched card.

In the textile industry most cloth is made by weaving. In weaving, two sets of yarns cross under and over one another at right angles.

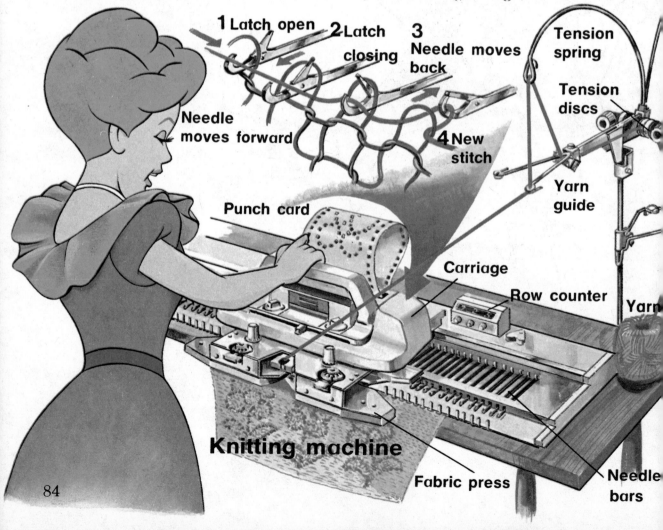

1 Latch open **2** Latch closing **3** Needle moves back

Needle moves forward

4 New stitch

Tension spring

Tension discs

Yarn guide

Punch card

Carriage

Row counter

Yarn

Knitting machine

Fabric press

Needle bars

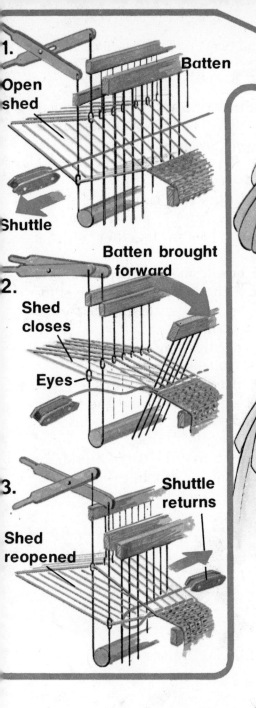

1.
Open shed

Batten

Shuttle

2.
Batten brought forward

Shed closes

Eyes

3.
Shuttle returns

Shed reopened

Hand loom

Hand levers

Healds

Warp beam

Shafts

Ratchets

Reed

Cloth Beam

One set of yarns (the warp) is threaded lengthways through the machine. The other set of yarns (the woof) is then threaded line by line through the warp yarns by a shuttle.

The warp yarns are parted to form an opening, or shed, for the shuttle to pass through. Some yarns go up; the others go down. They are moved by the healds. These are wires with "eyes" in the middle through which the warp yarns pass.

The inset diagram explains the sequence of weaving:

1. The healds are moved one way to form a shed, through which the shuttle is then passed.

2. The shed is closed, and the batten is moved forward to push, or "beat," the newly woven line firmly in place.

3. The healds are reversed to form another shed through which the shuttle is again passed to form another line of weave.

Speedy Sewing

A sewing machine is one of the house-wife's best friends. It enables her to attempt sewing tasks that would otherwise be beyond her or would take too long by hand. All sewing machines work in a basically similar way, though they vary a great deal in detail.

The simplest ones are worked by hand by turning a crank and handle, but most used today are powered by electric motors. They are switched on and off by a foot switch, which leaves both hands free to hold the fabric being stitched.

The workings of a machine look very complicated. There are all kinds of levers, linkages, shafts, cams (raised pieces on shafts) and drive belts. They are all accurately put together so that the threads from the needle to the bobbin intertwine at the correct time to form a stitch. The thread to the needle comes from a spool on top of the machine. The bobbin carries its own supply of thread.

The illustration opposite entitled "Making a Stitch" shows how the needle and bobbin together form a stitch.

1. The needle pierces the fabric and enters the bobbin area. The shuttle hook catches the needle thread as it turns.
2. The needle moves up while the hook continues turning.
3. The needle thread slips off the hook and goes around the bobbin thread.
4. The needle thread is pulled upwards by the thread take-up lever and the stitch, called a lock-stitch, is completed.

Even Stitching

For a neat finish, all stitches must be of the same length. This is brought about by the joint actions of the presser foot and the feed, which is a small toothed rack. The presser foot holds down the fabric layers while they are being stitched. The feed holds the fabric firmly against the presser foot while the stitch is being completed. Then it moves forward a precise amount to position the fabric for the next stitch.

The more expensive modern sewing machines are even more complicated, with extra shafts, levers and cams. They have needles that can move from side to side as well as up and down. Such "swing-needle" machines are used for making buttonholes and sewing on buttons. These machines also usually have feeds that can go backwards as well as forwards.

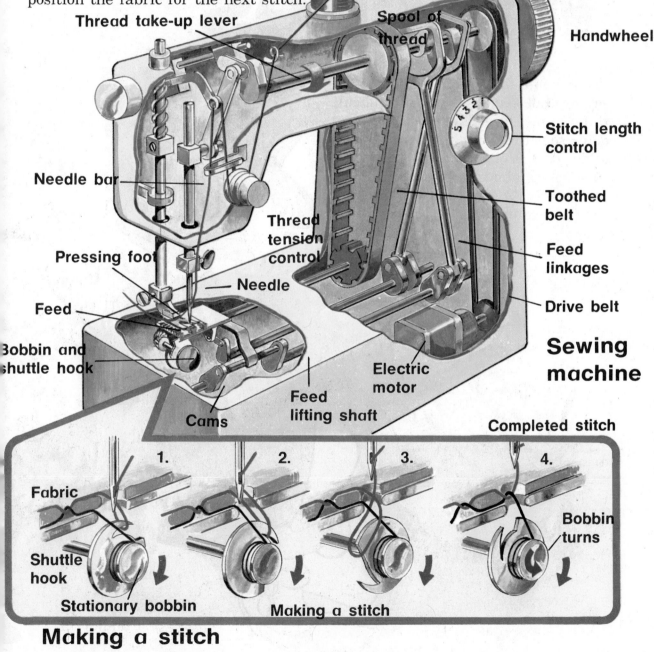

Thread take-up lever

Spool of thread

Handwheel

Needle bar

Stitch length control

Toothed belt

Pressing foot

Thread tension control

Feed linkages

Needle

Feed

Drive belt

Bobbin and shuttle hook

Sewing machine

Electric motor

Cams

Feed lifting shaft

Completed stitch

1.   2.   3.   4.

Fabric

Bobbin turns

Shuttle hook

Stationary bobbin

Making a stitch

Making a stitch

Clocks and Watches

"Time waits for no man" goes the old saying, but "time" is a very difficult thing to measure. When you are busy doing something you like, time appears to fly past. Yet when you are bored, time seems almost to stand still. You cannot rely on your senses to measure the passage of time.

Watch

Gnomon

Sundial

Tower clock

You have to rely upon something that happens very regularly. One thing that is regular is the daily movement of the Sun across the sky. Using a sundial you can tell the time by the position of the shadow of the pointer, or gnomon, but when the Sun goes in, you are in trouble!

The most reliable way of telling the time is with a clock or a watch. Clocks measure time by having something inside them which moves or vibrates steadily.

Lazy rooster

Clockwork

Before we look inside clocks, let us look inside some simpler things which work in much the same way. They include various mechanical toys which are driven by clockwork.

Like many clocks and watches, a clockwork toy is powered by a coil spring which takes the form of a thin steel ribbon. When you wind it up, the spring bends to form a tight coil. When you release the spring, it starts to uncoil. As it does so, it turns a gearwheel. The teeth on this wheel engage teeth on other gearwheels, which drive around a spindle or axle. In a simple clockwork mouse, the axle turns wheels which make the mouse move. In the "walking" bird shown below, the axle moves in a slot in the legs. The legs pivot back and forth and make the bird "walk."

By putting in different kinds of gearwheels all sorts of mechanical toys can be made, which can perform a variety of actions. Other effects can be incorporated too. A clockwork train, for example, may have a flint and striker to make sparks come from its funnel.

Clockwork toys

Return spring

Pivot

Slot

Power wheel

Coil spring

A music box makes music by means of clockwork. Its mechanism is nearer to that of a clock because it uses a regulator to help control the speed at which the spring uncoils.

When you wind up a music box, the spring becomes more tightly coiled. As it uncoils, it turns through gearwheels a cylinder on which there are projecting pins. As the cylinder rotates, the pins pluck thin metal reeds. When this happens, the reeds vibrate and give out musical notes. The reeds are each of different length and give out different notes. The pins are arranged around the drum so that they play a tune on the reeds.

A cog on the cylinder drives other cogs which spin around a kind of paddle. This spinning paddle helps to keep the cylinder turning at a steady speed. It is a simple kind of regulator, a device which is essential in clocks.

A simple wire pivot device is used in the music box to stop the mechanism. It is pushed in when the lid of the box is shut. In the box below a spindle holds the figure of a ballerina, which spins while the music is playing.

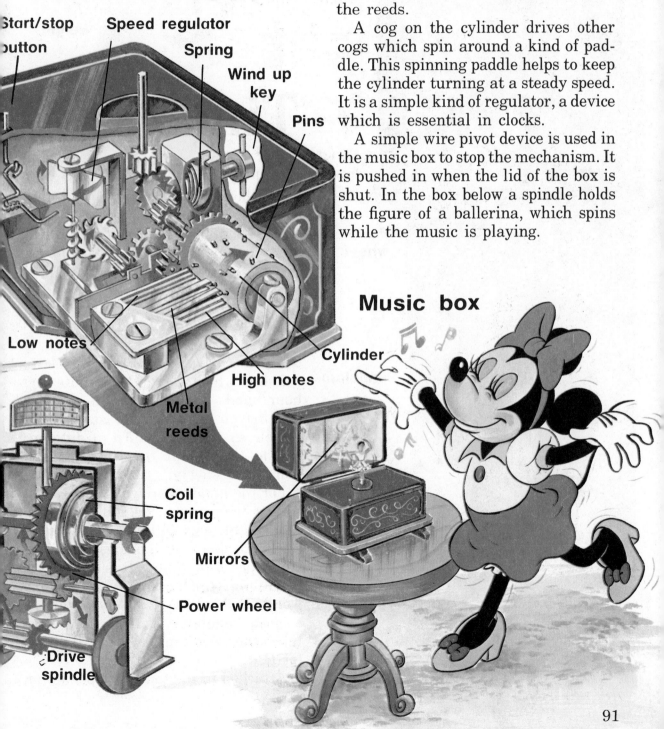

Start/stop button

Speed regulator

Spring

Wind up key

Pins

Low notes

High notes

Metal reeds

Cylinder

Coil spring

Mirrors

Power wheel

Drive spindle

Music box

Escape wheel

Anchor

Second hand

Hour hand

Weight

Gear wheel

Minute hand

Power wheel

Pendulum

Weight

Pendulum bob

Time Flies

Many clocks and watches are powered by coil springs, like clockwork toys are, but others are powered by falling weights. The tall grandfather clock is one of these. A cord or chain is wound around the axle of the power wheel, and at the end of this chain hangs a heavy weight. As the weight descends, the cord or chain unravels and turns the power wheel.

The movement of the power wheel is transmitted by toothed gearwheels to spindles which carry the minute and hour hands of the clock. The spindles are driven by different sized gearwheels so that they turn at different speeds, the minute hand fast and the hour hand slowly.

For the hands to move at the correct speeds, the power wheel must turn and the weight must fall at a steady rate. The clock therefore includes a mechanism called a regulator. It is a swinging pendulum, which is simply a rod with a weight (bob) at the end. A pendulum is a good regulator because it always takes the same time to swing back and forth.

Attached to the top of the pendulum

Bellows

Sound box

Anchor

Cam wheel

Cam lifts lever

Both bellows are opened

Lever falls holding second bellows away

Second bellows fall

Spring

Power wheel

To weights

escape wheel moves a second hand on the clock face.

Most grandfather clocks inform you of the time not only by their hands but also by chiming. They usually chime every quarter of an hour, each chime being different. On the hour they chime the number of hours. The chimes are triggered off when cogs in the clockwork mechanism turn past a certain point.

Other clocks "sing out" the time in a different way – as with the call of a cuckoo. A small bird appears through an opening at the proper time. The cuckooing and movement of the bird are both triggered off by the clockwork mechanism. The "cuckoo" sound is made by two bellows which are opened and closed by means of a propeller-like cam (see above).

rod is a two-pronged piece of metal called the anchor, because of its shape (see above). The prongs engage the teeth of a toothed wheel called the escape wheel, which connects with the clockwork mechanism. As the pendulum swings, the prongs pivot back and forth and allow the escape wheel to turn one tooth at a time. In many grandfather clocks this takes exactly one second, and the spindle of the

Automatic Timers

In England, one of life's greatest pleasures is an early morning cup of tea. Some homes have automatic timed tea makers.

At the heart of the tea maker is a kind of alarm clock. It not only has ordinary hour and minute hands, but also a pointer which you set to the time you want to be awakened. The water in the kettle is boiled by a heating element, as in an ordinary electric kettle. The kettle rests on a hinged platform with a spring beneath it. When it is full, it is heavy and holds the platform down. The platform presses in the button of a push switch. As the kettle empties, it becomes lighter. The platform springs up and releases the switch.

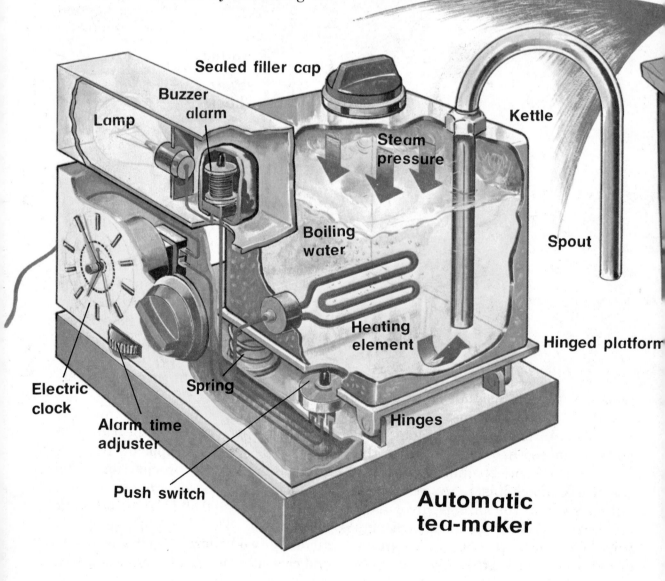

Sealed filler cap

Lamp

Buzzer alarm

Steam pressure

Kettle

Boiling water

Electric clock

Spring

Heating element

Spout

Hinged platform

Alarm time adjuster

Hinges

Push switch

Automatic tea-maker

This is what happens in the tea maker in the morning: About 10-15 minutes before the alarm is due to go off, a time switch turns on the heating element in the kettle. The water eventually boils, and some of it turns into steam. The pressure of the steam above the boiling water builds up and forces the water out through the spout and into the teapot. A safety valve in the kettle's filler cap opens if the pressure becomes too high.

After a minute or so, the kettle is almost empty and so light that the spring beneath the platform pushes the platform up. This releases the button of the push switch. Releasing the button causes the switch to turn off the kettle heater and turn on the buzzer and the light.

Time switches like the one in the automatic tea maker are used to do many other things in the home. They can turn on radios to wake you up in the morning. They can switch lights on and off at different times of the day and night.

Water Clocks and Watches

One of the earliest ways of measuring time was with a water clock. The one shown in the picture follows an ancient Roman design. Water drips from a tap at a steady rate into a receiving vessel. A cork floating in this vessel steadily rises as the water drips in. A cord runs from the cork around a drum, to which a pointer is attached. As the cork moves up, the drum turns and moves the pointer round the clock dial.

Even the best water clocks are not very accurate, however. For accurate timekeeping you need a modern watch. Some of the latest digital watches are accurate to a minute fraction of a second a day! Ordinary watches are accurate to a few seconds a day. They mostly have a coiled mainspring to power them, rather like clockwork toys. To regulate them, they have a balance wheel, a delicate wheel which spins back and forth at a steady rate. As it does so, it lets the escape wheel move one tooth at a time. The movement of the escape wheel is then passed by gearwheels to the hands of the watch.

Most ordinary watches have to be wound up by hand, but some are self-winding. They contain a swinging weight which is geared to the mainspring. Whenever you move your arm, the weight turns and winds up the spring.

Other watches have batteries to power them. Digital watches do, so do

Reservoir

Driving drum

Adjustment

Weight

Water clock

Float

Inventor

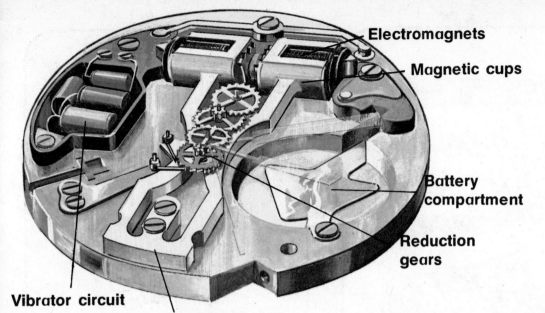

Electromagnets

Magnetic cups

Battery compartment

Reduction gears

Vibrator circuit

Tuning fork

Electronic watch

electronic watches. Electronic watches are regulated, not by a spinning balance wheel, but by a vibrating tuning fork. The tuning fork is set vibrating by battery operated electromagnets. The vibrations are then passed on to gearwheels which drive the hands of the watch.

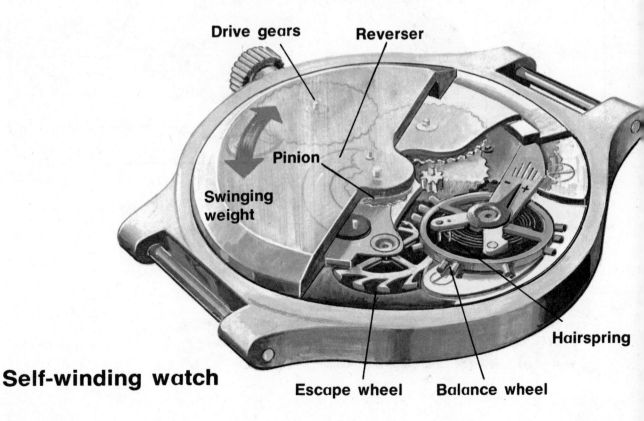

Drive gears

Reverser

Pinion

Swinging weight

Hairspring

Self-winding watch

Escape wheel

Balance wheel

Doors and Windows

When the first homes were built, many thousands of years ago, doors and windows were merely openings in the wall. Later wooden shutters were fitted over the windows, and wooden doors came into use.

The Romans first put glass in windows about 2,000 years ago, but only the richest Romans could afford to do so. Sometimes transparent sheets of mica (a kind of mineral) were used in windows instead of glass. Sheet glass for windows was very difficult to make until about two centuries ago. It could only be made in small sizes and distorted the light passing through it. Today window glass is cheap, perfectly clear, and can be made in huge sizes.

The Romans were also skilled locksmiths, but locks have been around since the days of ancient Egypt, protecting homes from intruders.

Aneroid barometer

Aneroid can

Pointer

Rack and pinion

Magnifying levels

Mortise lock

Return spring

Two-way latch lever

Latch

Lever springs

Stop

Levers

Bolt

Keyhole

Barometer

A barometer measures the pressure of the air all around us. This varies from day to day with the weather. When the air pressure is falling, the weather should get worse.

The usual kind of barometer found in the home is an aneroid (airless) barometer. It is so called because it contains a sealed can from which much of the air has been removed. When the pressure of the air changes, the top of the can moves in or out. This movement is magnified by levers, which turn a pointer that moves over a scale.

Cylinder lock

Springs

Drivers

Cylinder

Pins

Plug

Key

Locks

The most common kinds of locks used today are the lever, or mortise, lock and the pin-cylinder lock. In a typical mortise lock, one or more levers (or "tumblers") can pivot about a pin on the locking bolt. In the locked or unlocked position a notch on the inside of each lever engages with a bar, or stop, fixed to the lock body, and the bolt cannot move.

When the right key is put in the keyhole and turned, the key bit lifts the levers clear of the stop. As it continues turning, it moves the bolt backwards or forwards to unlock or lock. When the key is withdrawn, the notches engage the stop once more and prevent the bolt from moving. Some mortise locks are designed in a different way. For example, the stop may be fixed to the bolt and move through the slot in the levers.

The pin-cylinder lock is a modern version of the lock invented by the ancient Egyptians. The main part of the lock is a cylinder, which contains a plug that can turn when the correct key is inserted in it.

Inside the lock body are drilled five holes, which line up with holes drilled in the plug. These holes each contain two tiny rods (drivers and pins) of different sizes. In the locked position the pins and drivers project from the body into the plug, and prevent it from turning. When the correct key is put in the lock, the notches on the key lift the pins so that they are exactly level with the top of the plug. The plug can then be rotated, and the bolt moved.

Ding Dong Bell

Gong

Clapper

Electro-magnets

Adjustable contact screw

Spring

Battery

the trigger device by the side of the window are pressed together. Electricity flows from the power supply to the electromagnets and makes them magnetic. They attract a metal strip, or armature (dotted position).

When, however, the window is

Sometimes locked doors alone are not enough to protect your home from uninvited guests. Most burglars enter through the windows, for many windows can easily be forced. You can make the burglar's life more difficult by having window locks, which are hard to force. Or you can have a burglar alarm.

One simple alarm is shown in the picture. It is made up of two parts. One part consists of a switch that is triggered off when the window opens. The other is the alarm device. Both are worked by electromagnets, which are coils of wire that become magnets when electricity is passed through them.

When the burglar alarm is "on" and the window is closed, the contacts in

Contact open

Burglar alarm

Window opened

Electro-magnets

To power supply

Armature

176-7

opened, the contacts spring open. This cuts off the electricity to the electro-magnets, which thereupon lose their magnetism. The armature falls away on to another contact, which acts as a switch to the alarm bell.

With this switch on, electricty flows from the battery into the electro-magnets. They attract the armature, or clapper, which strikes the gong. As the clapper strikes, the spring moves away from the contact screw. The electric current is cut off, and the clapper and spring move back. As soon as the spring touches the contact screw, current passes again and the clapper is pulled on to the gong. In this way the gong is repeatedly struck.

The ordinary door "chimes" work in much the same way. The door bell switches on current to electromagnets which make a plunger strike a bar. The note it gives out causes a pleasant chime in a resonating pipe or chamber.

If your burglar is an expert lock picker, you can still foil him by wiring up a pressure pad under the door mat. When he steps on it, he triggers off an alarm bell. If he does manage to get inside, you can always rely on an ultrasonic alarm. This sends out sound waves so high-pitched that you – and he – cannot hear them. If he gets in the way of the beam, an alarm sounds.

Burglar

Door Bell

Guard dog

Wires to door bell

Chimes

Solenoid

Tone bar

Battery

Resonating chamber

Plunger

Louvered window

Glass
fixing springs

Vertical
link

Latch

Slat
opene[r]

Glass cutter

Cutting
wheel

Napping
slots

Windows

Most modern houses have large areas
of windows to make the inside as light
as possible. They may have huge picture windows that occupy most of one
wall. Ordinary house windows have
both fixed and opening sections, or
"lights." The opening windows may be
hinged at the sides or at the top.

A different kind of opening window
is the louvered window. In this the

Sash window

Pulleys

Sash cord

Sliding windows

Sash weight

glass is divided into several narrow slats, each of which can open. Louvered windows provide very good ventilation, and are often used in kitchens.

An older type of window has opening sections that slide up and down to open. They are called sash windows. The opening sections are specially balanced so that they stay open as much or as little as you wish. If they were not balanced, they would always fall downwards. They are balanced by means of lead weights, which hang on the end of sash cords attached to the top of each sliding window. The cord passes up and over pulleys in the top corners of the window frame.

The glass is usually fixed in windows by means of putty. This is a mixture of fine chalk and linseed oil. It is soft when applied but soon sets hard. In louvered windows the glass is fixed in rubber mounts by springs; but whatever method of fixing is used, the glass must be accurately cut. This is done by means of a glasscutter which cuts with a hard steel wheel.

Tuba

Trumpet

Concertina

Piano

Music stand

Double bass

Piano stool

Recording microphone

Headphones

Tape recorder

Sound and Vision

These days you don't need to leave your house to be entertained. You can listen to the radio, record player or tape recorder, or watch television. If you want to speak to someone in another town, you don't need to visit them. You merely have to call them on the telephone.

This is the Electronic Age, and all these devices work electronically. They work by controlling streams of tiny, invisible particles called electrons. Electrons are found in the atoms of all substances.

Indoor aerial

Old fashioned phonograph

Television

Play That Piano

One of the most popular musical instruments is the piano, or to give it its proper name the pianoforte. The word "pianoforte" means "soft-loud," because a piano can be played soft or loud.

The piano can be played with other instruments in a group or orchestra, but its wide range of notes and rich, full sound also make it an ideal solo instrument. The piano is classed as a keyboard instrument because you sound the notes by striking keys. When you depress a key, levers in the part of the piano called the action make a padded hammer strike a taut string.

The string, which is made of steel wire, then vibrates and sends out a musical note.

Actually each hammer strikes two or three strings at a time to produce a note. The ordinary piano usually has

Damper

Hammer

Roller

Screw

Spring

Key

Check

Hammer

Strings

Damper lever

Backcheck

Key

Upright piano

Top door

Lid

Loud pedal

Bottom door

Keyboard

Soft pedal

88 notes and about 230 strings. To make different notes, the strings are of different lengths. They are long for low notes and short for high notes. They are all held firmly in a very strong cast-iron frame.

The strings pass over a piece of wood called the bridge, which is fixed to a wooden sheet called the soundboard. This vibrates when the strings do and serves to strengthen, or amplify, the sound.

String

In the upright piano the strings are mounted vertically. In the grand piano used for concerts, they are strung horizontally, and most sound comes out through the open lid of the piano. Both the upright and grand pianos have pads called dampers in the action. These are normally pressed against the strings. When a key is struck, however, the damper is moved away from the string so that it can vibrate. When the key is released, the damper presses against the string once more and silences it. By pressing a pedal, you can deliberately hold the dampers away from the strings. Then all the strings carry on vibrating for much longer, producing a much louder sound. By pressing another pedal you can increase the damping effect on the strings so that the overall effect is quieter.

Lid

Strings

Case

Keyboard

Grand piano

We've Got Rhythm

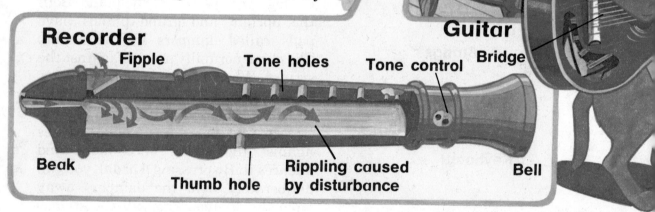

Mouthpiece

First valve slide

Finger ring

Second valve slide

Third Valve slide

Popular among the many other kinds of musical instruments are the recorder, the trumpet, the guitar and the drums. The recorder and trumpet are classed as wind instruments because air is blown through them. The guitar is a stringed instrument whose strings are plucked. The drum is a percussion instrument – one that is struck to make a noise. So is the cymbal.

The recorder is one of the simplest instruments, and is usually made of wood. It is really a kind of elaborate whistle. When you blow through the mouthpiece, you set up vibrations in the air inside the recorder body, and the vibrating air gives out a note. By

Guitar

Bridge

Recorder

Fipple

Tone holes

Tone control

Beak

Thumb hole

Rippling caused by disturbance

Bell

putting your fingertips and thumb over different holes in the body, you can make the air vibrate in different ways so that it gives out different notes.

The trumpet is a brass instrument. It consists of a long tube formed into coils. It has a cup-shaped mouthpiece at one end and a bell-shaped flare at the other. It also has a number of valves. By pressing the valves, the player can make the air go through a different length of tubing. In this way he can produce different notes. He can also produce different notes by altering the shape of his lips and varying the pressure of his breath. The bugle is a similar instrument, but with no valves.

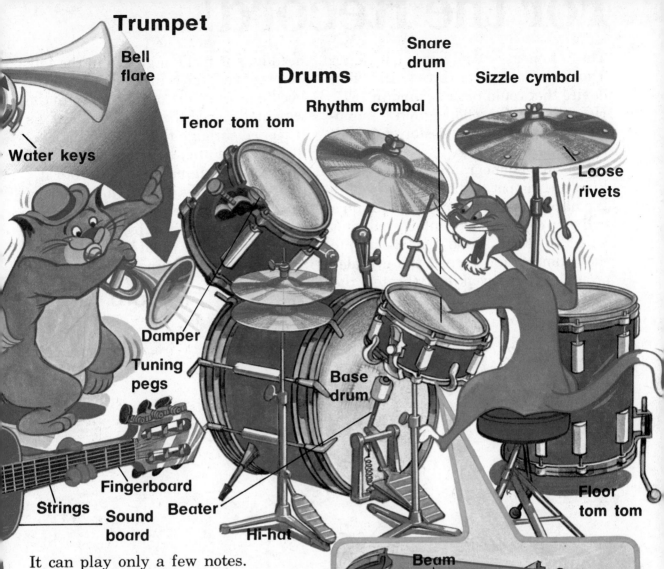

Trumpet

Bell flare

Water keys

Drums

Snare drum

Sizzle cymbal

Rhythm cymbal

Tenor tom tom

Loose rivets

Damper

Tuning pegs

Base drum

Fingerboard

Strings

Sound board

Beater

Hi-hat

Floor tom tom

Beam

Snare release trigger

Snares

It can play only a few notes.

The guitar produces music when its strings are plucked. The player plucks them either with the fingers or a plectrum. Most guitars have six strings, which give out different notes when plucked. The player can get many other notes from each string by pressing the string against the fingerboard. This effectively shortens the length of the string and so changes the note it gives out. From time to time the player has to "retune" the guitar by tightening or loosening the strings by means of the tuning pegs on the end of the fingerboard.

For sheer noise, drums and cymbals take some beating! Drums are simply cylinders or bowls with a skin (drumhead) stretched over one or both ends. Calfskin is generally used. The noise the drum gives out depends on the size of the skin, and how taut this skin is. Cymbals are brass discs which are beaten with a drumstick or crashed together.

For the Record!

The famous American inventor Thomas Edison produced the first device that could record sound in 1877. He called it the phonograph ("soundwriter"). It was the ancestor of today's record player.

Edison's phonograph consisted of a kind of trumpet with a needle fixed to the narrow end. The needle rested on a cylinder covered with tinfoil (and later wax). To record sound, you spoke into the trumpet and turned the cylinder around. Your speaking vibrated the needle as it made a groove in the foil. To play back the sound, you placed the needle at the start of the groove in the wax and turned the cylinder again. As it passed through the grooves, the needle vibrated and the trumpet gave out the sounds originally spoken into it.

Grooves are still cut in a modern record by a needle, and the "sound" is still taken from them by a needle, but the record is now a flat plastic disc not a tinfoil or wax cylinder.

Record player

The left-hand wall operates the left speaker

Groove of the stereophonic record

The right-hand wall operates the right speaker

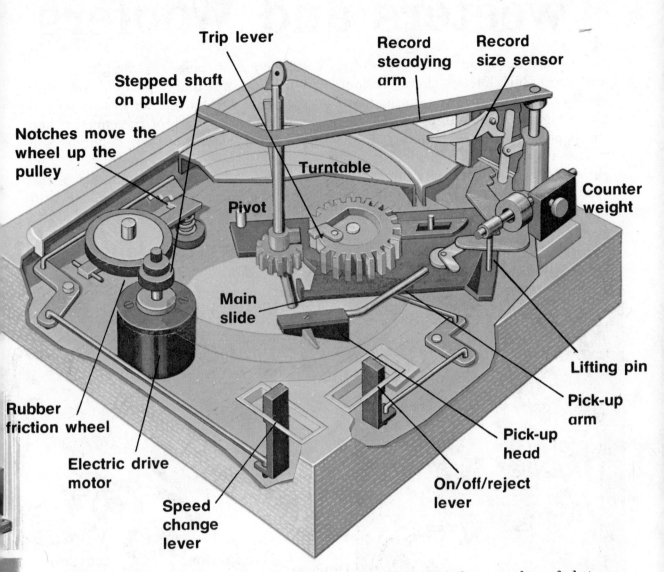

Trip lever

Stepped shaft on pulley

Record steadying arm

Record size sensor

Notches move the wheel up the pulley

Turntable

Pivot

Counter weight

Main slide

Rubber friction wheel

Lifting pin

Pick-up arm

Electric drive motor

Pick-up head

Speed change lever

On/off/reject lever

In the modern record player, the record is spun around on a turntable at a very precise speed. Long-playing (LP) records need to turn at exactly $33\frac{1}{3}$ revolutions per minute (rpm). Extended-play (EP) records need to turn at exactly 45 rpm.

The needle, or stylus, is set in a pick-up head, also called the cartridge. When it travels along the wavy grooves of a record, the stylus starts to vibrate. A magnet or crystal in the pick-up head changes the vibrations into tiny electrical signals. These signals then go to an electronic device called an amplifier, which strengthens the sig-

nals. The signals are then fed to a loudspeaker, where they are changed into sounds. These sounds are exactly the same as those which the recording artists made in front of the microphone at the recording studio.

Recordings are generally made using two or more microphones positioned to the right and left of the artists. They pick up slightly different sounds, which are recorded on opposite sides of the record groove. When the record is played back through lefthand and righthand speakers, the sounds are much more realistic. This is called stereophonic sound.

Tweeters and Woofers

No, we are not about to describe birds and dogs, but loudspeakers! A loudspeaker is a device which changes electrical signals into sound waves. It is the opposite of a microphone.

The usual kind of loudspeaker is called a dynamic, or moving-coil speaker. It works on a simple electromagnetic principle. When an electric current passes through a wire, which is in a magnetic field, the wire moves. It will move more or less according to the strength of the current, and it will move back or forth depending on the direction of the current.

The largest part of a speaker is the horn or cone, which is made of stiff paper. Fixed to the narrow part of the

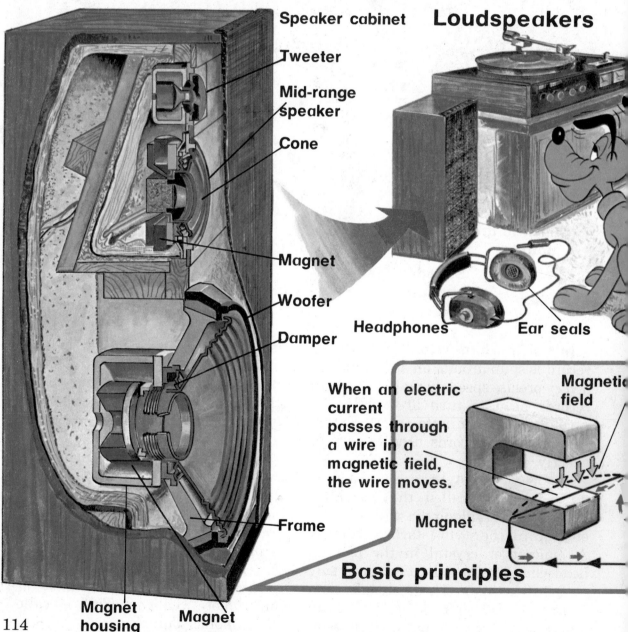

Loudspeakers

Speaker cabinet

Tweeter

Mid-range speaker

Cone

Magnet

Woofer

Damper

Headphones

Ear seals

Frame

Magnet housing

Magnet

When an electric current passes through a wire in a magnetic field, the wire moves.

Magnetic field

Magnet

Basic principles

cone is a short paper tube. Around this is wound a coil of wire. The tube is located inside a magnet. When electric current passes through the coil, the magnet makes the coil move, but the coil is attached to the tube, and the tube is attached to the cone; so when the coil moves, it causes the cone to move also.

The electrical signals from a tape recorder or record player are fed to the coil. They are continually changing, making the cone vibrate back and forth. These vibrations cause sounds to come from the speakers.

Headphones are really miniature speakers, which fit over the ears. They have a soft plastic seal around the outside so that they fit snugly and prevent outside noises getting in.

For best quality, or high-fidelity (hi-fi) reproduction of sound from a record player or tape recorder you need a number of loudspeakers. You need a

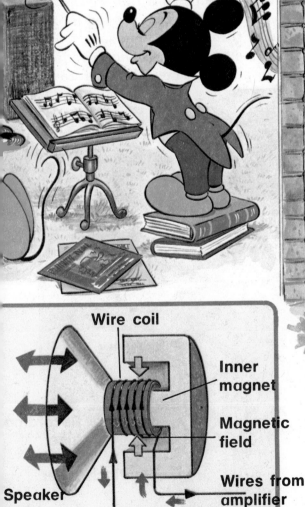

Wire coil

Inner magnet

Magnetic field

Wires from amplifier

Speaker cone

small speaker for the high notes, this being called a tweeter. You need a mid-range speaker for in-between notes. For the low, resonant notes you need a large diameter speaker, which is called a woofer. Usually all three speakers are housed in the same cabinet. An electronic device sorts out which of the incoming electrical signals go to which speaker to reproduce the various notes.

Getting It Taped

The small cassette tape recorder is taking over from the record player as the favorite way of playing recorded music. In a tape recorder, sounds are recorded as an invisible magnetic pattern on a special tape. Below you see a regular size tape recorder, which has the tape wound on quite large external spools. Opposite is the more portable cassette recorder, which has a narrow tape enclosed in a pocket-size cassette.

The tape used for recording consists of a plastic ribbon coated with either iron oxide or chromium oxide. These materials are unusual because they can be magnetized.

What happens in a tape recorder is this. Electrical signals are fed into the recorder through an input socket. They may come from a microphone, radio, or record player. They then go to the

Tape recorder

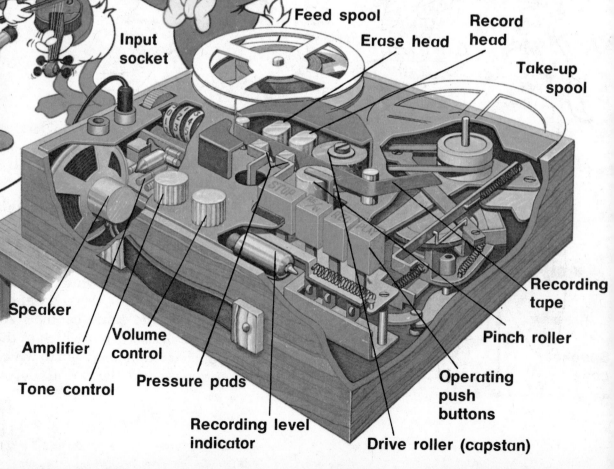

Input socket

Feed spool

Erase head

Record head

Take-up spool

Speaker

Amplifier

Volume control

Tone control

Pressure pads

Recording level indicator

Recording tape

Pinch roller

Operating push buttons

Drive roller (capstan)

"record head," which is a very sensitive electromagnet. This changes the electrical signals into magnetic ones.

Running past the record head is the tape. The magnetic signals from the head rearrange the particles in the coating on the tape into an invisible pattern. This pattern forms the recording.

To play back the recording, the tape is rewound and then moved past the record head, which also acts as the "play-back" head. This time the electromagnet in the head works in the opposite way. It picks up the magnetic signals from the tape and changes them into electrical ones. These electrical signals go through an amplifier, which makes them stronger. Then they are fed to a loudspeaker, which changes them into sound.

To prevent one recording being made on top of another, the tape goes past an "erase" head before the record head. The erase head removes any pattern there might be on the tape.

One of the commonest microphones used today is the crystal microphone shown below. When you speak into it, the sound makes the thin metal diaphragm vibrate. These vibrations squeeze a special kind of crystal. When this happens, the crystal gives out tiny electric currents. They represent the sounds that entered the microphone.

Microphone

Shield
Diaphragm
Crystal
Metal plates
Wires to recorder input
Casing

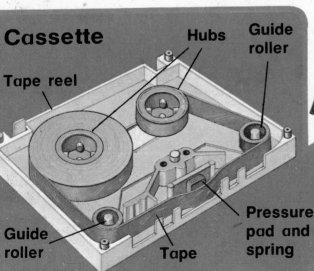

Cassette

Hubs
Guide roller
Tape reel
Guide roller
Tape
Pressure pad and spring

Radio Broadcasting

It is a mystery to many people how voices and music can be transmitted through the air and received on their radios. This is how it is done. First the sounds to be transmitted are changed by a microphone into electrical signals.

These signals can travel through wires but not through the air. The only things that can travel through the air, and also through space, are radio waves.

Radio waves belong to the same "family" of waves as light rays and heat rays. Like sea waves they ripple up and down, but they do it invisibly. Radio waves are much longer (from crest to crest) than light and heat rays.

Transmitting aerial

Broadcasting station

Radio waves

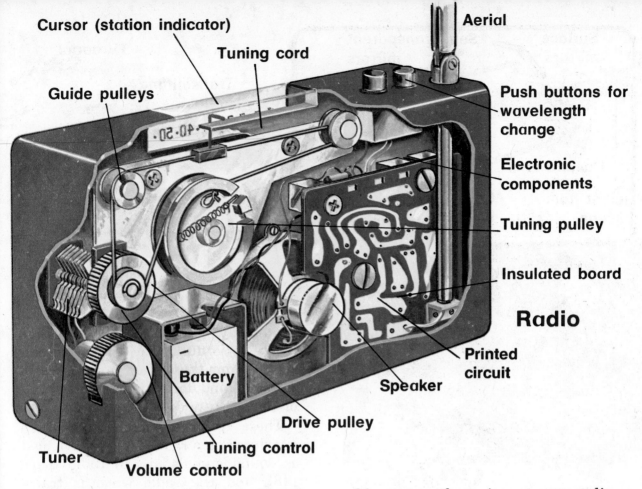

Cursor (station indicator)

Tuning cord

Aerial

Guide pulleys

Push buttons for wavelength change

Electronic components

Tuning pulley

Insulated board

Radio

Battery

Printed circuit

Speaker

Drive pulley

Tuning control

Tuner

Volume control

We say they have a longer wavelength.

At a broadcasting station the electrical signals from the microphone are made to alter a radio wave. The altered radio wave is then transmitted. Because it "carries" an imprint of the microphone signals, it is called a carrier wave. The carrier wave spreads out in all directions from the transmitting aerial. It can be picked up by the aerial of your radio receiver.

The receiver has electronic circuits containing components such as transistors. The circuits are able to remove the microphone "imprint" from the carrier wave and change it into electrical signals. These are then amplified, or strengthened, and fed to a loudspeaker. The speaker reproduces the sounds that went into the distant microphone.

Of course, there is not one radio wave being sent out by broadcasting stations, but many. A radio takes care of this by having a tuner. This changes the electronic circuits slightly so that they can detect radio waves of different wavelengths. The radio can then receive different programs. The tuner is linked by pulleys to a pointer, or cursor. This moves over a dial marked in wavelengths, and often broadcasting stations as well.

In many radios these days the electronic components are joined together by a printed circuit. This is an insulated board which has the circuit connections made on it by a printing technique. They consist of a thin film of copper, rather than the copper wire that was once used.

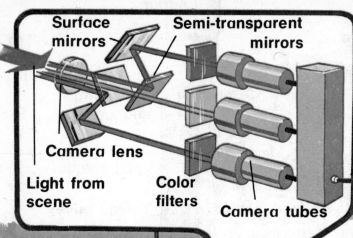

Color TV camera

Surface mirrors

Semi-transparent mirrors

Camera lens

Light from scene

Color filters

Camera tubes

TV aerial

Transmitting aerial

Pictures Through the Air

To understand the principles of the television camera and the picture tube, we shall deal first with simple black-and-white television transmission. In the camera, an electrical image is formed of the scene it views. This image is then scanned, or crossed, by a beam of electrons. The beam moves from one side to the other, then flicks back and down a little before moving across again.

As the electron beam strikes the electrical image, it triggers off a tiny electric current. Where the image is bright, the current is stronger than where it is dull. The electric signals coming from the camera thus represent the light and dark shades in each line of image scanned.

These picture signals are then imprinted on a radio carrier wave, just as sound signals are in radio (page 118), and the radio wave is transmitted.

Your television aerial picks up the wave and feeds it to your television receiver. The electronic circuits in the receiver remove the picture signals from the carrier wave and send them to the picture tube. In this tube an electron gun "fires" a beam of electrons at a fluorescent screen, which glows when electrons hit it. The beam is deflected by plates, and scans in exactly the same way as it did in the camera. Its brightness is altered by the picture signals, and a picture is built up on the screen, line by line, of light and dark shades. The process happens so quickly that your eyes see the picture as a whole.

In color television the camera splits up the scene viewed into the three basic colors – red, green, and blue – by

Deflecting coils

Three electron guns

Blue beam

Green beam

Red beam

Shadow mask

Resin

Protective window

Faceplate

Picture tube

Speaker

Color receiver

Shadow mask

Phosphor dot screen

Faceplate

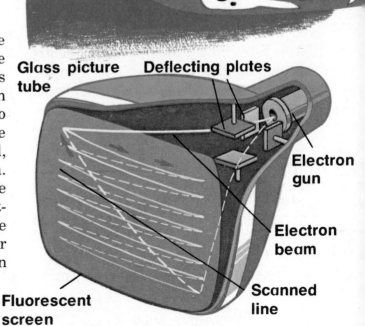

Black and white TV

means of mirrors and filters. These colors form images in three separate camera tubes. The three color signals are then transmitted. In the television receiver, the color signals are fed to three electron guns. The screen is made up of groups of dots which glow red, green or blue when electrons hit them. A shadow mask is arranged near the screen so that only electrons representing red can strike red dots, green strike green, and so on. In this way a color picture is built up as the electron beams scan the screen.

Glass picture tube

Deflecting plates

Electron gun

Electron beam

Scanned line

Fluorescent screen

Dial and Talk

Alexander Graham Bell made his famous invention of the telephone in 1876. Now you can speak by telephone to people in cities in almost every country in the world. The telephone changes your voice into electrical signals, which travel along the telephone lines to the people you are calling. Their telephone then changes the signals back into sounds.

The parts of the telephone which change sound into electrical signals and electrical signals into sound are housed in the receiver, which you pick up. The mouthpiece houses the mic-rophone, or transmitter. It contains a thin metal diaphragm which presses against a mass of granules of carbon held in a brass cup. An electric current passes through the granules. When you speak into the mouthpiece, your voice makes the diaphragm press against the carbon granules with variable pressure. This alters the electric current passing through them. In this way the vibrations made by your voice are changed into a variable current.

It is this same current, when amplified, which travels down the telephone lines to the receiver of the person you are calling. It travels to his earpiece. There it passes through the coils of small electromagnets, and makes their magnetism vary. In front of the electromagnets is a thin metal diaphragm which moves back and forth as the magnetism varies. The diaphragm vibrates the air to recreate the sounds that went into the caller's mouthpiece.

You contact the person you want by dialing.

You put a finger in the appropriate hole in the fingerplate, rotate it around to the stop, and then let go. A spring returns the fingerplate to its original position. As the fingerplate returns, it drives around a train of gears. The last gear has a cam (raised piece) attached to it. Each time it turns around, it opens two contacts, which cause a pulse of electricity to be transmitted down the telephone line. As many pulses are transmitted as the number you dial. These pulses operate equipment in the telephone exchange, which connects your telephone with that of the person you are calling.

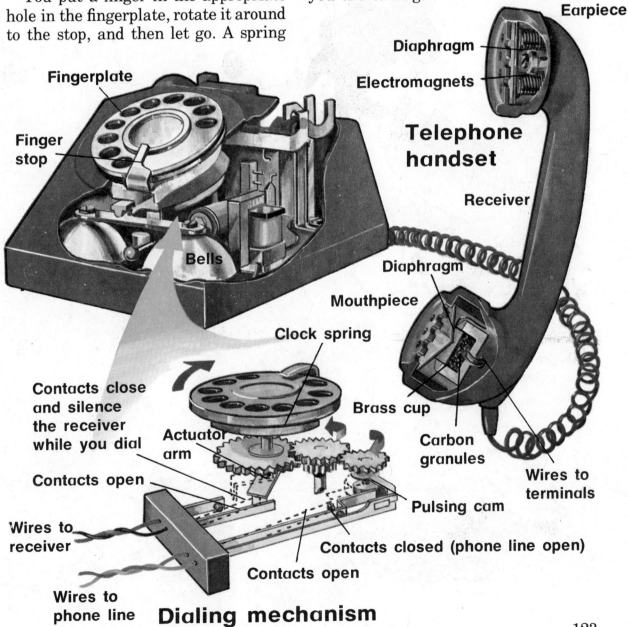

Earpiece

Diaphragm

Electromagnets

Telephone handset

Receiver

Fingerplate

Finger stop

Bells

Diaphragm

Mouthpiece

Clock spring

Contacts close and silence the receiver while you dial

Contacts open

Actuator arm

Brass cup

Carbon granules

Wires to receiver

Wires to terminals

Pulsing cam

Contacts closed (phone line open)

Contacts open

Wires to phone line

Dialing mechanism

Out of Doors

In many homes a great deal of activity also goes on out of doors. There is nearly always something to be done in the garden, particularly in the growing season. There is ground to be dug, seeds to be sown, plants to be looked after, lawns to be mowed and hedges to be trimmed.

If you don't feel like gardening, why not do some carpentry instead? Or mend your bicycle? Or perhaps you would prefer to sit in your garden swing, watch the fountain play, and let somebody else get on with the work!

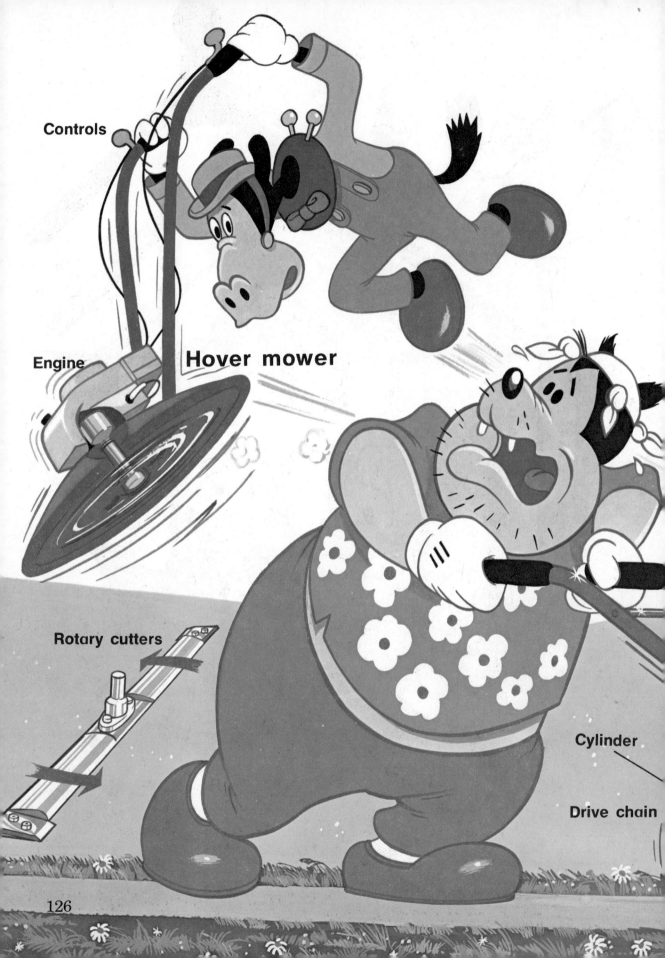

Controls

Engine

Hover mower

Rotary cutters

Cylinder

Drive chain

Mowing and Blowing

From the spring until the autumn everything grows rapidly in the garden – particularly the grass! In a wet warm summer it can grow 2 inches (5 cm) or more in a week. Mowing the lawn is therefore one of the regular jobs to be done in the garden. If you want to lose weight, try a hand mower. By pushing this up and down, you will lose pounds!

The usual kind of machine is the cylinder mower shown below. This has a heavy cylinder at the rear, which helps roll the ground and also drives the cutter blades around. The grass is cut as it is caught between the cutter blades and the cutter bar. The height of the cutter bar is adjusted by moving the front roller up or down.

For speed and ease of cutting, a power mower is needed. It may be driven by electricity from a battery or from a socket. The most popular is driven by a gasoline engine. Some powered mowers are cylinder machines. Others are rotary machines. They each have a cutter bar that is spun rapidly around and around hundreds of times a minute.

One kind of rotary mower blows air downwards to lift it a few inches above the ground. It floats, or hovers, on a "cushion" of air, in much the same way that a hovercraft or air-cushion vehicle does.

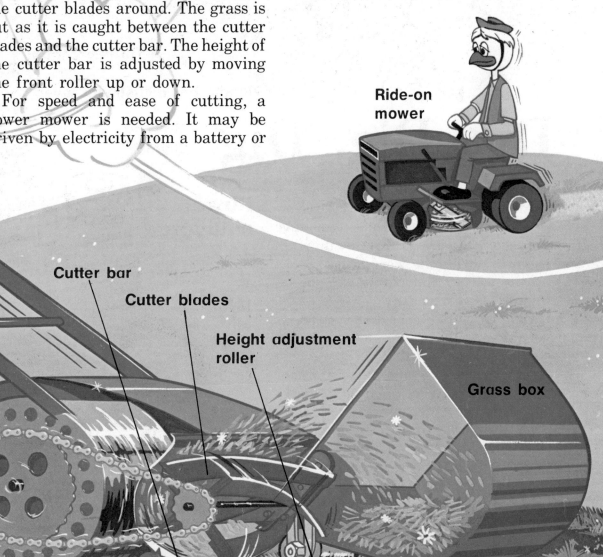

Ride-on mower

Cutter bar

Cutter blades

Height adjustment roller

Grass box

Dig, Dig, Dig

One of the most common chores in the garden is digging. Whatever you grow – flowers, fruit or vegetables – you have to prepare the ground first by digging. Digging buries the weeds and breaks up the soil so that plants can spread their roots more easily.

Digging with an ordinary spade is very slow and very strenuous. It is also "backbreaking" because of the way you bend your back as you lift a spadeful of soil. One way of avoiding back-ache is to use a mechanical spade. You push the spade into the ground, and then pull down on the handle. The blade springs up, carrying with it the soil, without placing any strain on your back.

Throttle control

Handle bar adjustment lever

Starting handle

Power cultivator

Engine

Clutch roller

Drive belts

Fuel tank

Wheels

Gearbox

Depth control bar

Rotor blades

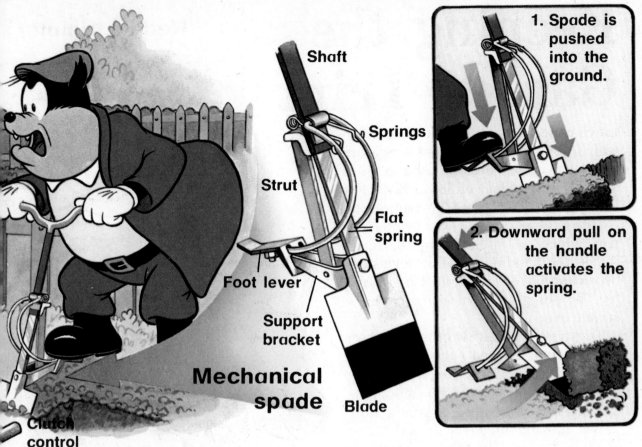

Shaft

Springs

Strut

Flat spring

Foot lever

Support bracket

Mechanical spade

Blade

Clutch control lever

1. Spade is pushed into the ground.

2. Downward pull on the handle activates the spring.

Using a mechanical spade is easier than hand digging, but not much quicker. For speed you need a power digger. Power diggers usually do many things besides digging, including hoeing and weeding. So they are usually called cultivators. "Cultivating" means digging, hoeing and weeding the ground you are using to grow plants.

The power cultivator shown here is fitted with shaped rotor blades for digging. It has a small gasoline engine, which is started by pulling the starter. The handle of the starter is joined to a tough cord. This is wound around a wheel on the drive shaft of the engine. When you pull the cord, you turn the engine over until it "fires" and starts. You control the speed of the engine from a throttle on the handlebars.

The engine drives around a pulley, and twin drive belts connect this pulley to another pulley in the front of the cultivator. The second pulley turns the shaft to the gearbox. Gears in the gearbox reduce the engine speed and drive the rotor blades around at about 100 times a minute.

The gearbox is disconnected from the engine by means of the clutch. When you pull the clutch lever, the clutch roller moves and loosens the drive belts so that they no longer grip the engine pulley.

For hoeing and weeding, you can take off the rotor blades and replace them with a pair of drive wheels. You place a frame carrying the hoeing tools behind the engine, and the drive wheels pull it through the ground.

Keeping the Garden Trim

Lawn mowers cut the grass on the lawn well in most places, but not so well in awkward places such as around trees and along the edges of flower beds. For this job you need an edge trimmer.

One edge trimmer works by electricity, which is supplied by batteries inside the handle. These batteries can be recharged, or "refilled with electricity," by plugging them into an electric socket overnight.

The trimmer has two blades, like a pair of clippers, and each has several teeth. The top blade moves from side to side on top of a fixed bottom blade. Cutting is with a kind of scissor action.

The moving blade is driven by an electric motor through a series, or train, of gears. The last gearwheel in the train has a pin attached to it. This pin fits into a slot in the rear of the moving blade. When the gearwheel turns, the pin moves up and down the slot, pushing the blade from side to side.

Hedges as well as lawns need attention in the growing season. This can be done most quickly with an electric hedge trimmer. It works in much the same way as the edge trimmer just described, with one fixed and one moving blade. Hedge trimmers may be battery or electrically operated.

The leaf sweeper is another useful gardening aid. It has a rotating brush which sweeps the leaves into a basket. The brush is driven by gears from the sweeper wheels.

Hedge trimmer

Moving blade

Fixed blade

Motor

Gear train

Pivot

Edge trimmer

130

Drive gears

Motor

Brushes

Moving blade

Fixed blade

Leaf sweeper

Collection basket

Roller

Drive pinion

131

Sprinkling and Spraying

For plants to grow well they must have plenty of water. Gardeners can use a hose or a sprinkler.

A sprinkler has one or more arms with holes in it, which are moved around by water pressure. They spray water from the holes as they move. The sprinkler shown here is made to rotate by a simple water turbine. The incoming water spins around the turbine wheel as it passes through to the spray arm. The wheel is connected by gears to linkages that move the spray arm in a wide arc.

Another common kind of sprinkler has twin spray arms with angled nozzles at each end. When the water is turned on, it spurts out of the nozzles in such a way that the arms spin around.

Water sometimes forms a more permanent feature of the garden, such as a pond. Ponds not only look nice, they also attract many forms of water life. They can be made even more appealing by adding a fountain. A pump takes water from the pond and forces it through a nozzle up into the air. An electric motor spins the pump, which consists of a disc with vanes on it. The whole unit should be well insulated to

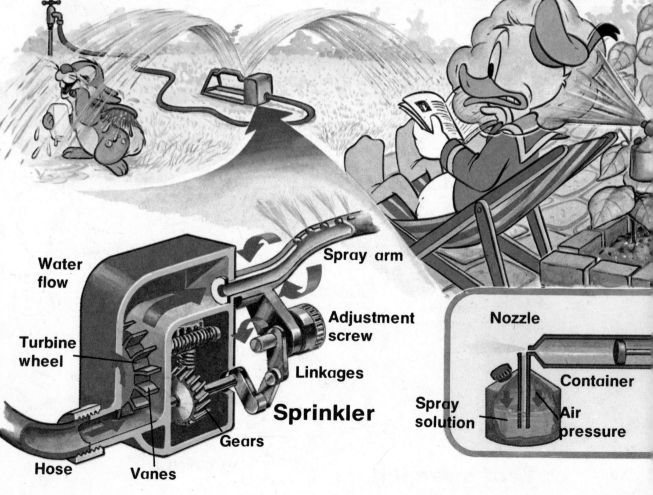

Water flow

Spray arm

Adjustment screw

Turbine wheel

Linkages

Sprinkler

Gears

Hose

Vanes

Nozzle

Spray solution

Container

Air pressure

Fountain pump

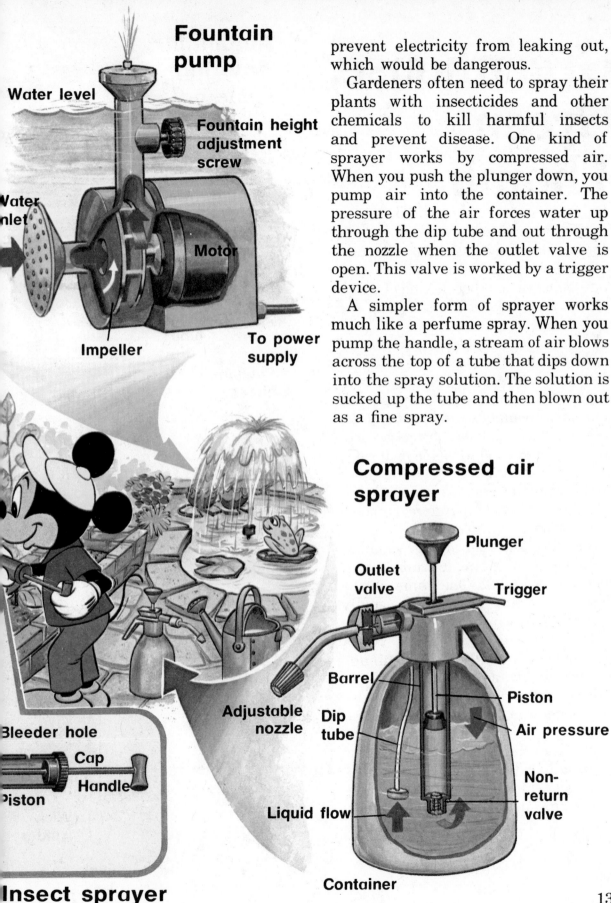

Water level

Fountain height adjustment screw

Water inlet

Motor

Impeller

To power supply

prevent electricity from leaking out, which would be dangerous.

Gardeners often need to spray their plants with insecticides and other chemicals to kill harmful insects and prevent disease. One kind of sprayer works by compressed air. When you push the plunger down, you pump air into the container. The pressure of the air forces water up through the dip tube and out through the nozzle when the outlet valve is open. This valve is worked by a trigger device.

A simpler form of sprayer works much like a perfume spray. When you pump the handle, a stream of air blows across the top of a tube that dips down into the spray solution. The solution is sucked up the tube and then blown out as a fine spray.

Compressed air sprayer

Plunger

Outlet valve

Trigger

Barrel

Piston

Adjustable nozzle

Dip tube

Air pressure

Liquid flow

Non-return valve

Container

Bleeder hole

Cap

Handle

Piston

Insect sprayer

133

Greenhouse, Green Thumb

Gardeners can grow a wider variety of plants when they have a greenhouse, also called a glasshouse or a hothouse. A greenhouse is a special kind of building made mainly of glass to trap the sun's heat.

Putting it simply, a greenhouse works because the sun's rays can pass readily through glass, while heat rays cannot. Sunlight passes through the glass of a greenhouse and heats up the objects inside. As these objects become hotter, they give off invisible heat rays, which cannot escape through the glass. They remain trapped inside the greenhouse, which therefore becomes very warm.

The sides and roof of a greenhouse are made up of a simple frame which holds panes of glass. The frame may be of wood or metal. The wood is usually cedarwood, which contains natural oils that prevent it from rotting. Metal greenhouses are made of aluminum, which is light and does not rust.

Because the plants in a greenhouse are under cover, they must be watered regularly. This can be done by hand using a watering can, or automatically. In an automatic watering system the plant pots stand on a spongy matting, which dips into a trough containing water. The matting soaks up moisture and keeps the plants watered from the

Automatic watering system

Water tank

Supply tube

Polythene sheet

Matting

Kerosene heater

Hot air

Supply trough

Chimney

Window

Fuel gauge

Wick winder

Fuel tank

Filler cap

Automatic vent opener

Adjustable rod

Power cylinder

Lever arm

Control valve

bottom. The supply trough is kept filled from a water tank at a higher level.

You can also use a device to help keep the greenhouse cool in hot weather. It is an automatic vent opener, which is fitted to the vents in the roof. It consists of an arrangement of rods and levers which are connected to a cylinder containing liquid. When the temperature rises, the liquid expands and forces the lever arm to move. This pushes the vent open. When the temperature falls, the liquid in the cylinder shrinks, the lever arm drops, and the vent is pulled shut.

In very cold weather the greenhouse may need to be heated to prevent the plants inside dying. Kerosene or electric heaters may be used. Electricity is also used to heat propagators in which seedlings are raised. They are miniature greenhouses which are heated by coils embedded in the soil.

Seed tray

Peat

Gravel

Thermostat control

Heating coils

Heat Sensor

Propagator

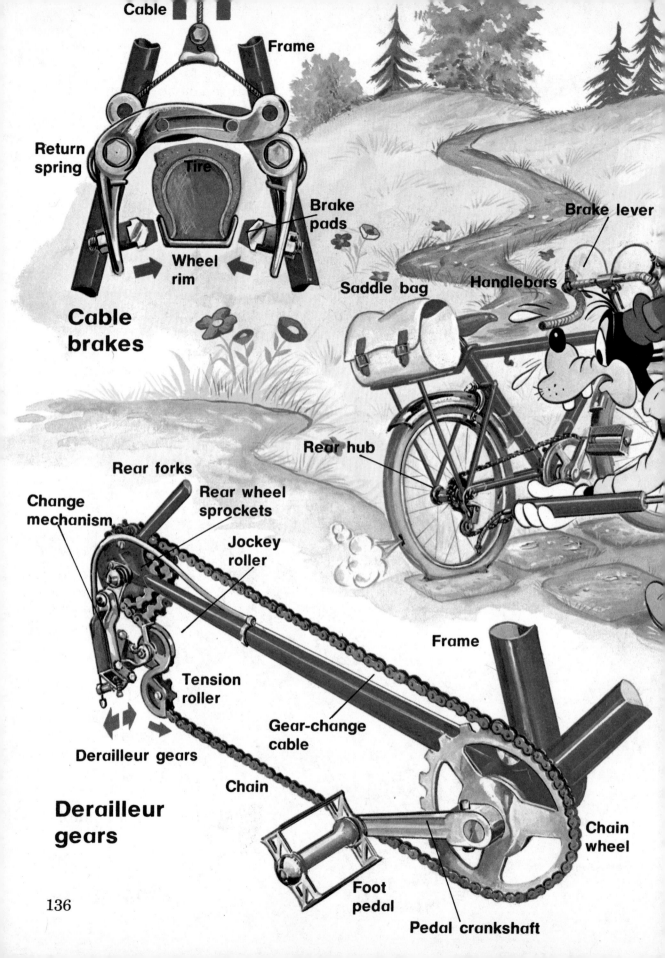

Cable

Frame

Return
spring

Tire

Brake
pads

Wheel
rim

**Cable
brakes**

Brake lever

Saddle bag

Handlebars

Rear hub

Rear forks

Rear wheel
sprockets

Change
mechanism

Jockey
roller

Tension
roller

Frame

Gear-change
cable

Derailleur gears

Chain

**Derailleur
gears**

Chain
wheel

Foot
pedal

Pedal crankshaft

Two-Wheelers

One machine we are all familiar with is the bicycle. It puzzles some people how you can ride a bicycle so easily without constantly overbalancing. The secret lies in the movement of the bicycle wheels. When a wheel is spinning, it tends to remain pointing in the

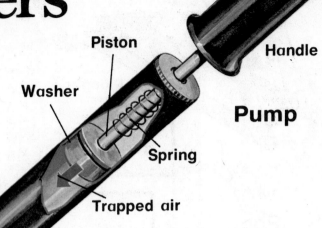

Pump

Piston

Handle

Washer

Spring

Trapped air

Adapter

Air flow

Valve

Wheel rim

Air in

Tire

same direction, so when you start pedaling with the wheels upright, the wheels will tend to remain upright as long as they keep turning.

The frame of a bicycle is made up of lengths of steel tubing welded together. Each wheel usually has a steel rim, which is linked by spokes to a hub in the center. The rim is covered by a pneumatic, or air-filled tire. The air is contained in a thin rubber inner-tube beneath a tougher outer covering.

The wheels fit into front and rear forks. They are held there by nuts that screw on to a spindle that runs through the hub. There are ball bearings on each side of the spindle which allow the hub to turn around it. The front fork is held in bearings within the main frame so that it can be moved from side to side for steering.

The pedal crankshaft turns in bearings too. It carries the cranks and pedals and also on one side a toothed chainwheel. An endless chain connects the chainwheel to a smaller sprocket on the rear hub. As you pedal, you turn the chainwheel and the chain makes the rear wheel turn too. Some bicycles have three or more rear sprockets of different sizes. This gives them three or more gears. A gear-change mechanism (derailleur) beneath the sprockets moves the chain from one to another when you move the gear-change lever. Other bicycles have a hub gear. A large rear hub contains gearwheels of different sizes. They move together in different ways to make the hub turn at different speeds.

Valve

Pedal

Bleeder hole

Plunger

Air sucked into cylinder

Return spring

Valve closed

Foot pump

Tools for the Job

With the cost of motoring rising higher and higher, it is sensible to do some simple jobs on your car yourself. One thing you should do at least once a week is check the pressure of the air in your tires. Your car will not "hold the road" well if the tires are too flat or too hard.

You test the tires with a pressure gauge. The head of the gauge is pressed over the tire valve. The pin in the valve is pushed down, allowing air into the gauge. The air presses against a plunger, which is forced backwards against a spring. It moves more or less according to the pressure of the air. As the plunger moves, it pushes out an indicator. The tire pressure can be read from the scale on the indicator.

If the pressure in your tires is too

Combination wrench

Socket wrench brace

Adjustable wrench

Screwdriver

Head

Spring

Seal

Pin

Plunger

Tire valve

Air pressure

low, you will need to pump them up. For this you will need a foot pump. This has a pedal which you press down to pump air into the tires. On the downward stroke of the pedal, the pump body moves past the plunger. Air is drawn in through the bleeder hole. When the pedal is released, the spring returns the pedal to its original position. Air passes through a valve into the space in front of the plunger. On the next downward stroke this air is forced by the plunger from the air outlet and into the tire.

When you have a puncture, however, you have to change the wheel. First, however, you have to raise the wheel off the ground with a jack.

The car jack shown works by hydraulic (liquid) pressure. When you work the handle back and forth, air is pumped through a one-way valve into the liquid chamber. It pushes against the liquid, which in turn forces out the plunger. This causes the beam to rise and lift the car. When you want to let the car down, you press the release pedal. This opens the release valve, which lets the air escape from the liquid chamber, and the plunger goes back into the chamber.

Among the most useful tools you need to work on your car are wrenches, with which you do up and undo nuts. There are ordinary open-ended wrenches, ring wrenches and box wrenches. Particularly useful is a set of socket wrenches. This consists of different sized "heads" which fit on to the end of a ratchet handle or brace.

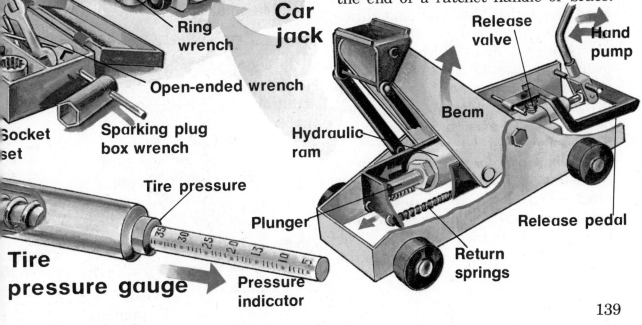

Ring wrench

Car jack

Open-ended wrench

Release valve

Hand pump

Socket set

Sparking plug box wrench

Hydraulic ram

Beam

Tire pressure

Plunger

Release pedal

Tire pressure gauge

Pressure indicator

Return springs

Handyman

When things need fixing around the house or in the garden, it is handy if you can do them yourself, but you will need quite a number of tools to do the jobs properly. Almost certainly you will often be called upon to drill holes for screws, not only in wood but in metal, brick or concrete. Then you will need an electric drill.

It must be plugged into an outlet. It has a powerful motor switched on and off by a trigger switch in the pistol-grip handle. The drill bit (the part that does the drilling) is held in jaws that are opened and closed by a chuck. The chuck itself is tightened by means of a chuck key. This has teeth cut in it which match the teeth on the side of the chuck.

The drill shaft is linked by gear-wheels to the drive shaft of the motor. Often more than one set of gears are used which allow the drill to run at several speeds. A fan is fitted on the drive shaft to blow air through the motor, which would otherwise become too hot. Both shafts are mounted in bearings so that they run smoothly.

You can fit a variety of attachments to most electric drills which make them even more useful. These may be a circular saw, polisher, wire brush, grindstone and sander. With a sanding device you can smooth rough wood or remove old paint.

Another way of removing old paint is by using a blowtorch. With a blow-torch you burn the paint off. A few years ago you would have used a blow-lamp, which burned kerosene. The blowtorch of today, however uses the liquid gas propane. Propane is one of the gases in natural gas, which is found in the ground near oil deposits. By applying pressure to propane, you can liquefy it and then bottle it. When you reduce the pressure on the liquid, it changes back into gas.

The blowtorch is a unit that screws on to a gas canister. As it does so, it pushes down a valve in the top of the canister, which allows the gas inside to escape. The gas passes up into the torch head through another valve, which is opened by a control knob. As the gas flows through the head, it sucks in air through the intake holes. The gas and air form a mixture that burns with a very hot flame.

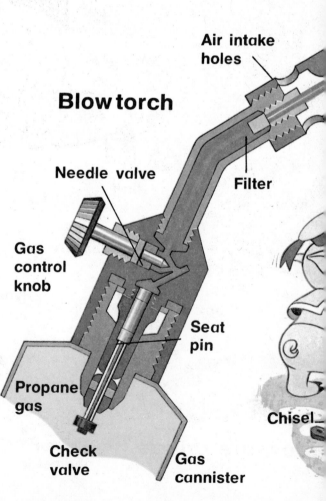

Drill bit

Blowtorch

Air intake holes

Needle valve

Filter

Gas control knob

Seat pin

Propane gas

Check valve

Gas cannister

Chisel

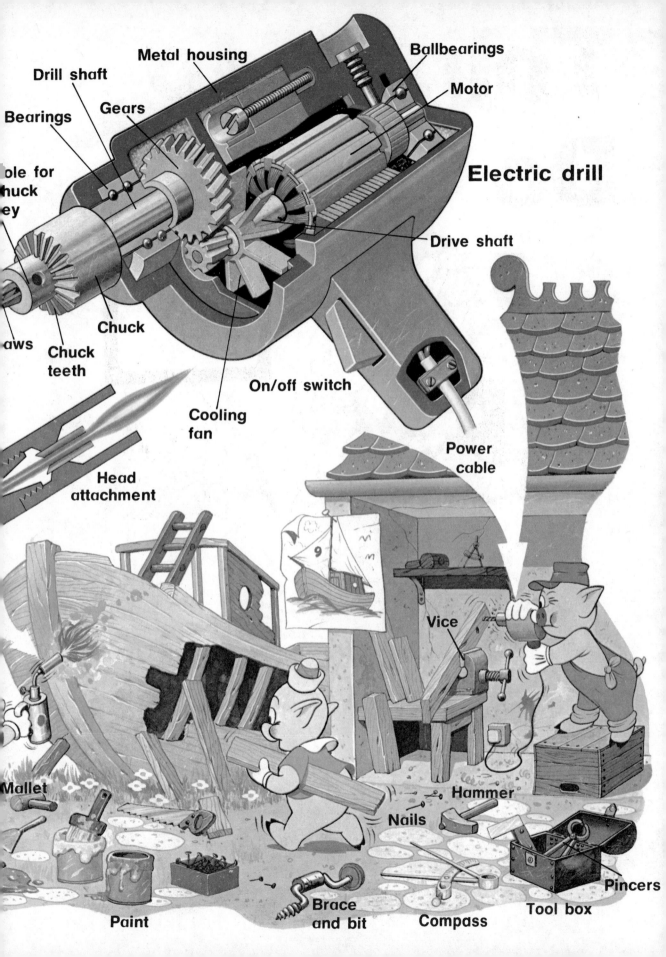

Electric drill

Drill shaft

Metal housing

Ballbearings

Gears

Bearings

Motor

ole for
huck
ey

Drive shaft

aws

Chuck

Chuck
teeth

On/off switch

Cooling
fan

Head
attachment

Power
cable

Vice

Mallet

Hammer

Nails

Pincers

Paint

Brace
and bit

Compass

Tool box

Things to Do

Screen

Projector

Audience

Projectionist

Film strip

Filmspool

142

There is no shortage of things to do at home in your spare time. The problem is rather finding time to do them all. Collecting hobbies are very popular, and people collect all kinds of things from matchboxes, coins and stamps to butterflies and rocks and minerals. You will find many of your nature specimens much more interesting if you examine them under a magnifying glass or a microscope.

Photography is another rewarding hobby. Even with the simplest camera you can take good pictures. You can not only take pictures out of doors, but also indoors in your own "studio". If you have a movie camera you can make your own "movies". Then you can show them at home, as long as you can thread the film through the projector properly!

Background scenery

Floodlight

"Birdie"

Model

Camera

Film roll

Tripod

Binoculars

Photographer

Telescope

Magnifying glass

Photograph album

Taking Pictures

It is nice to have photographs of places you have visited and people you have met, and taking photographs has never been easier. Even the simplest cameras you can buy will take good pictures.

Basically a camera is a light-tight

Reflex camera

Film wind lever

Shutter button

Shutter speed scale

Viewfinder

Pentaprism

Rewind lever

Focusing ring

Motor

Feeding claw

Filmgate

Disc shutter

Camera lens

Film

Film transport sprocket

Reflex mirror

Self-timer lever

Iris diaphragm

Movie camera

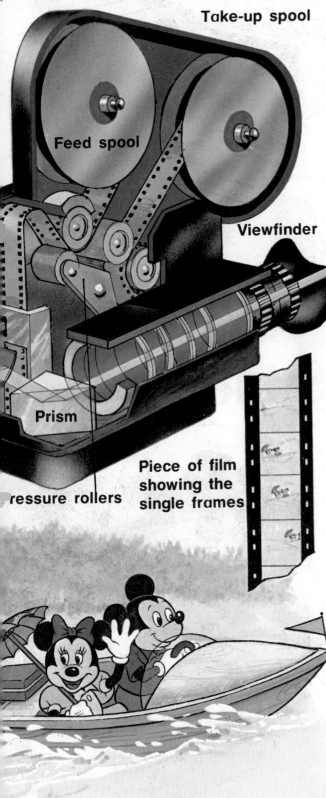

Take-up spool

Feed spool

Viewfinder

Prism

ressure rollers

Piece of film showing the single frames

box with a lens in one side and a piece of film opposite. A shutter is needed to cover the lens when you are not taking photographs. When you open the shutter for an instant, the lens throws an upside-down picture of the scene outside on to the film. The light changes chemicals in the coating on the film. These changes can be made visible during the process of developing, and converted by printing into a picture of the scene you photographed.

With simple cameras you don't have to worry about focusing your lens to make the picture sharp, and your camera will perform quite well as long as the light is good. With more complicated cameras like the one in the picture you can take better pictures if you work the controls properly. There are controls for focusing the lens, for changing the time the shutter is open, and for varying the size of the lens opening, or aperture. The device that changes the aperture is the iris diaphragm.

This camera is a single lens reflex camera. It has a mirror that reflects light from the lens into the viewfinder when you are composing the picture. The mirror flips out of the way when the photograph is taken.

The movie camera takes moving pictures, or at least appears to. What it actually does is take separate still pictures in rapid succession. The film is wound continuously from one spool to the other, but it is held still in the film gate when the shutter opens. The shutter is a spinning disc with a piece cut out. After exposure, the shutter turns and covers the film gate, and it is then that the film is wound on. This ensures that no blurring occurs.

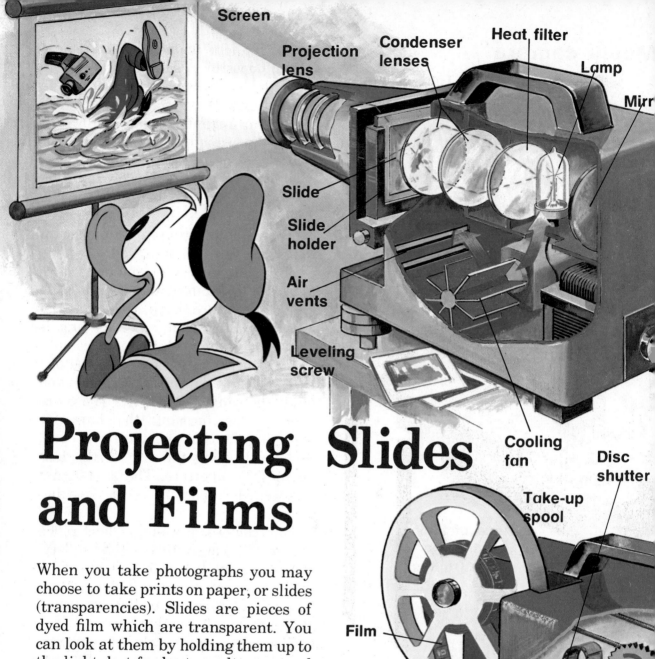

Screen

Projection lens

Condenser lenses

Heat filter

Lamp

Mirr

Slide

Slide holder

Air vents

Leveling screw

Cooling fan

Projecting Slides and Films

When you take photographs you may choose to take prints on paper, or slides (transparencies). Slides are pieces of dyed film which are transparent. You can look at them by holding them up to the light, but for best results you need to project them on to a screen, when you can make them much larger.

In a simple slide projector a curved mirror reflects the light of a powerful lamp through the slide. A lens then throws an enlarged image of the picture in the slide on to the screen. The lens is focused to make the picture sharp. A fan is included in the projector to blow cool air over the lamp,

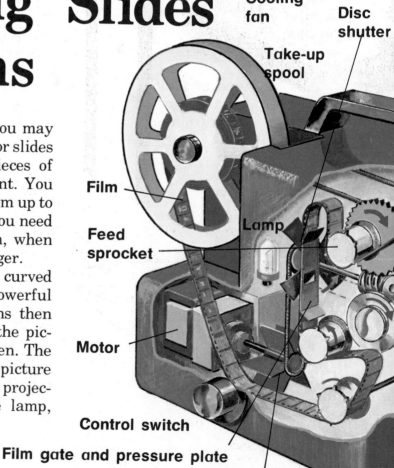

Disc shutter

Take-up spool

Film

Lamp

Feed sprocket

Motor

Control switch

Film gate and pressure plate

Cooling fan

which would otherwise overheat and break down.

In this projector the slides are placed in the holder one by one. Other projectors use holders that contain many slides. They have a simple mechanism for feeding the slides in as required.

The movie projector has a similar kind of optical system to the slide projector. It has a mirror and lamp, and a lens to throw a magnified image on to the screen. The film is wound continuously through the projector from one spool to the other, but it has to be projected while it is still, otherwise blurring would occur.

So the film is fed through the film gate one little picture, or frame, at a time. It is held still for a fraction of a second while light is passed through it. Then the disc shutter rotates and cuts off the light, while the film advances another frame. This frame is projected in turn.

The movie projector projects 24 frames on to the screen each second. Each frame shows a slight change from the one before it. Our eyes hold on to the image of one frame as they see another. (This is called persistence of vision.) The result is that our eyes see a gradually changing image in which objects appear to move.

Slide projector

Film spool

Spring drive belts

Drive chains

Projection lens

Movie projector

Leveling screw

Writing

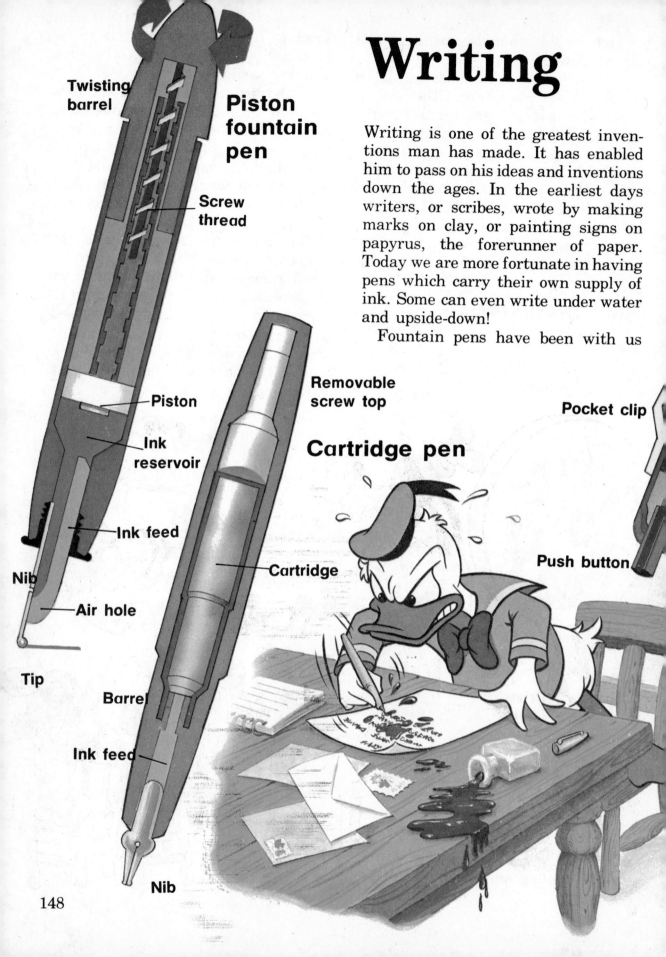

Twisting barrel

Piston fountain pen

Screw thread

Piston

Ink reservoir

Ink feed

Nib

Air hole

Tip

Barrel

Ink feed

Removable screw top

Cartridge pen

Cartridge

Nib

Pocket clip

Push button

Writing is one of the greatest inventions man has made. It has enabled him to pass on his ideas and inventions down the ages. In the earliest days writers, or scribes, wrote by making marks on clay, or painting signs on papyrus, the forerunner of paper. Today we are more fortunate in having pens which carry their own supply of ink. Some can even write under water and upside-down!

Fountain pens have been with us

Ball point

Coil spring

Barrel

Socket

Ball

Spring stop

Ink tube

Ball point pen

Rotable guide

Plunger

now for nearly 100 years. Two kinds are shown here. One holds its ink in a reservoir (tank) formed by the body of the pen. It has a piston which is screwed up to fill the reservoir. The ink is sucked into the pen through the air hole in the point.

Another kind of fountain pen is the cartridge pen. The ink is contained in a replaceable plastic container, or cartridge that pushes into the base of the pen. Another kind of pen has a reservoir like a sponge. To fill it, you simply dip the point into ink, which is then soaked up.

When you write with a fountain pen, ink flows from the reservoir through the narrow channel of the ink feed. It flows underneath the point and down the slit to the tip. There it is transferred to the paper. As the ink slowly flows out of the reservoir, air slowly flows into it through the air hole. The points of fountain pens are often made of a gold alloy. They are tipped with a very hard metal, such as iridium, to make them hard-wearing.

Another very popular pen is the ball point pen. It writes with a special thick ink, which dries almost instantly. In the writing tip of the pen is a tiny steel ball, held in a socket. When not in use, the ball seals the ink tube. When you write, the ball rolls and carries with it a thin film of ink.

The ink reservoir and writing tip form a separate unit which is mounted inside the body of the pen. Another unit, or refill, can usually be put in when the first has run out of ink. Many ball point pens have a device such as a push button to retract, or pull in the writing tip when the pen is not being used.

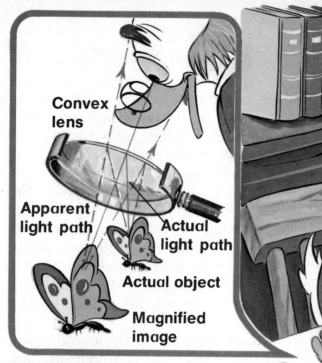

Convex lens

Apparent light path

Actual light path

Actual object

Magnified image

Magnifying glass

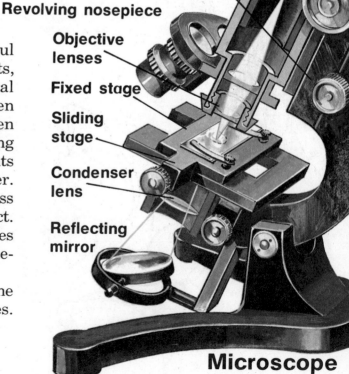

Eyepiece

Drawtube

Body tube

Fine focusing adjustment

Revolving nosepiece

Objective lenses

Fixed stage

Sliding stage

Condenser lens

Reflecting mirror

Larger than Life

The world about us is full of beautiful things – colorful plants and insects, cuddly animals and sparkling mineral crystals. Many of these things are even more beautiful and interesting when you look at them under a magnifying glass or microscope. These instruments magnify, or make things appear larger.

Their lenses – curved pieces of glass – bend the light coming from an object. It is bent in such a way that it makes the eye believe it comes from something much bigger.

A magnifying glass has only one lens. A microscope has several lenses.

Microscope

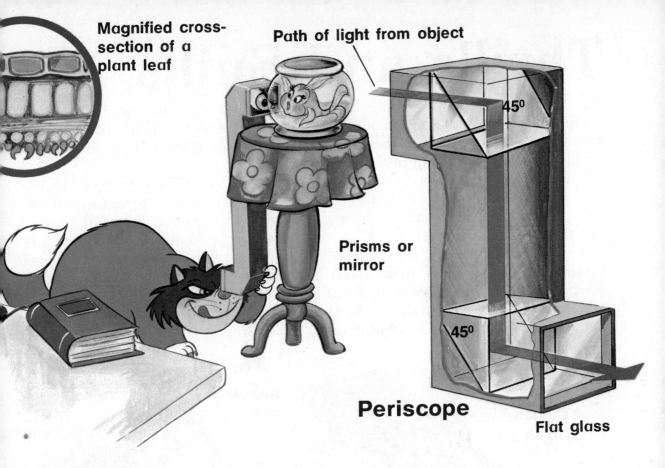

Magnified cross-section of a plant leaf

Path of light from object

45⁰

Prisms or mirror

45⁰

Periscope

Flat glass

Main focusing adjustment

The main lenses of the microscope are those in the eyepiece (at the top) and in the objective (at the bottom). The eyepiece is mounted so that you can move it up and down. You do this to focus on the object you are examining, that is, produce a sharp picture of it.

With a microscope you can look at the surface of something, or you can slice something very thin and look through it. You put the object you wish to examine on a piece of glass called a slide. You then clip the slide to the sliding stage, which you can move along the fixed stage. If you are looking at something transparent, you shine light through it by way of a mirror. This is what is happening in the picture.

With another kind of "seeing" instrument you can look round corners and over high walls. It's like having your eyes on stalks! This instrument is the periscope. Submarines have periscopes so that their crew can look out of the water while they are still submerged.

A periscope has a long body tube with openings at top and bottom on opposite sides, as shown in the picture. In the openings are slanted mirrors or prisms. They are angled so that light entering one opening is reflected along the tube and then out of the other opening.

151

Thrills and Spills

Not many of us will actually be a racing driver but with a little imagination we can capture some of the Grand Prix excitement by racing model cars. The cars are powered by electricity and run along a track which can be formed into smooth corners, tight bends, underpasses and overpasses.

A typical track has two racing lanes, around which two cars can be raced. Each car has a guide blade in front which fits into a groove in the track. At the sides of the guide are flexible metal contacts which pick up electric current from metal strips on the track. Wires from the contacts lead to an electric motor.

When electric current flows to the motor, the shaft, or armature, of the motor spins around. A small toothed wheel, or pinion, on the armature drives around a toothed gearwheel attached to the car's rear axle, and so the car is propelled.

The electricity to power the cars comes from a transformer. This takes

Electric cars

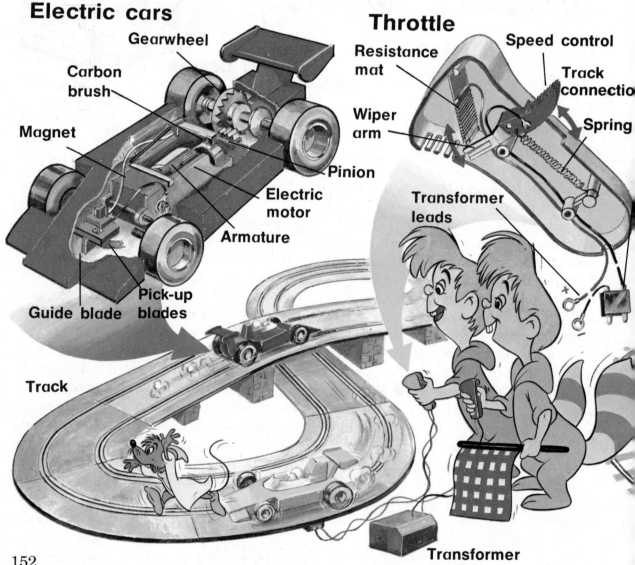

Gearwheel

Carbon brush

Magnet

Guide blade

Pick-up blades

Pinion

Electric motor

Armature

Track

Throttle

Resistance mat

Wiper arm

Speed control

Track connection

Spring

Transformer leads

Transformer

152

electricity from the socket and reduces it to a safe voltage. The amount of electric current passed to the track is controlled by a hand throttle. The greater the current, the faster the car will go. The throttle has a trigger which moves an arm across a special coil of wire. This wire is called resistance wire. When the arm moves across the coil, more or less of the wire becomes included in the electric circuit to the track, and the current falls or rises as the case may be.

Electric train sets work in much the same way as the racing cars just described. The picture shows how one kind of engine works. The railroad track can be made interesting by introducing crossover tracks, level-crossings, tunnels and shunting yards. The points, which switch a train from one line to another, are worked by a simple electromagnet, so are the level-crossing gates. The diagram below shows how they work. When electric current is passed through the coil, the coil becomes a magnet and attracts the iron core. This works the gate.

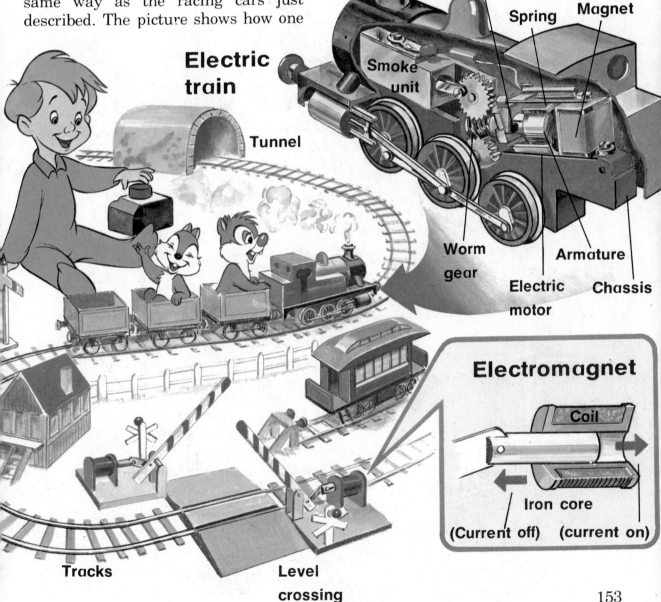

Electric train

Carbon brush

Spring

Magnet

Smoke unit

Tunnel

Worm gear

Armature

Electric motor

Chassis

Electromagnet

Coil

Iron core

(Current off)   (current on)

Tracks

Level crossing

Index